ABOUT OMEGA

Omega was founded in 1977, a time when holistic health, psychological inquiry, world music and art, meditation, and new forms of spiritual practice were just budding in American culture. Omega was then just a small band of seekers searching for new answers to perennial questions about human health and happiness. The mission was as simple as it was large: to look everywhere for the most effective strategies and inspiring traditions that might help people bring more meaning and vitality into their lives.

Since then, Omega has become the nation's largest holistic learning center. Every year more than 25,000 people attend workshops, retreats, and conferences in health, psychology, the arts, and spirituality on its eighty-acre campus in the countryside of Rhinebeck, New York, and at other sites around the country. While Omega has grown in size, its mission remains the same. Omega is not aligned with any particular healing method or spiritual tradition. Its programs feature all of the world's wisdom traditions and are committed to offering people an opportunity to explore their own path to better health, personal growth, and inner peace.

The name Omega was inspired by the writings of Teilhard de Chardin, a twentieth-century mystic and philosopher who used the word to describe the point within each one of us where our inner spiritual nature meets our outer worldly nature. Teilhard believed that the synthesis of these two domains presented the greatest challenge—and the greatest hope—for human evolution. Of his belief in the balance between world and Spirit, Teilhard wrote, "I am going to broadcast the seed and let the wind carry it where it will."

Omega has taken on the task of helping spread that seed so that a better world for all of us can continue to take root and grow.

The Omega Institute
Mind, Body, Spirit Series

An Omega Institute Mind, Body, Spirit Book

The Power
of Ritual

Rachel Pollack

A DELL TRADE PAPERBACK

A DELL TRADE PAPERBACK

Published by
Dell Publishing
a division of
Random House, Inc.
1540 Broadway
New York, New York 10036

Written by: Rachel Pollack
Series Consulting Editor: Robert Welsch
Series Editor: Kathleen Jayes
Series Manager: James Kullander
Literary Representative: Ling Lucas, Nine Muses and Apollo Inc.
Illustrations by: Howard R. Roberts (HROBERTSD@aol.com)

Dell books may be purchased for business or promotional
use or for special sales. For information please write
to: Special Markets Department, Random House, Inc.,
1540 Broadway, New York, NY 10036.

DTP and the colophon are trademarks of Random House, Inc.

Library of Congress Cataloging in Publication Data
Pollack, Rachel.
    The power of ritual / Rachel Pollack.
       p.   cm. — (The Omega Institute mind, body, spirit series)
    Includes index.
    ISBN 0-440-50872-X
    I. Ritual—Psychology.   I. Title.   II. Series.
  BL600.P65 2000
  291.3'8—dc21   99-038831

Printed in the United States of America

Published simultaneously in Canada

January 2000

10 9 8 7 6 5 4 3 2 I
RRD

BOOK DESIGN BY JENNIFER ANN DADDIO

Omega Institute sends out heartfelt thanks and appreciation to staff members and teachers for their support and contribution in the preparation and publication of this book.

Contents

Part Four: Ritual and You

The Power

of Ritual

Introduction

Rituals are ceremonies done to connect us with the world around us and with the energy that flows through all existence. They can be as simple as lighting a candle alongside a photo of a sick relative, or as elaborate as a hundred people in bright costumes dancing, drumming, and singing on the longest day of the year. Ritual allows us to experience nature in intense and personal ways. We do not just look at the Moon and think how beautiful it looks. We celebrate it. Ritual is serious, but it also is creative, and can be enjoyed by people of all ages. Children love to paint banners, gather wildflowers, or build a bonfire. As we shall see, rituals often involve feasting, with special symbolic foods. For all its sensuous joy, ritual also gives us a framework to allow our deepest feelings to emerge and then share them with others.

Ritual draws on the wisdom and knowledge of thousands of years. And yet it does not mean blindly following the examples of others. We may look to older cultures and contemporary teachers for inspiration—and we will do a great deal of that in this book—but we always make ritual more real by making it our own.

In the West, technology and economics have dominated most of the twentieth century. In the United States, especially since World War II, when we speak of "the good life," we mean a home of our own, vacations, possessions, good clothes. We understand that we need love and family to truly benefit from these things, but "the good life" is primarily an economic expression. As the twentieth century ended, however, we began to question this materialist view. Suppose a "good life" meant a life filled with wonder, with intimate knowledge of the divine, with an expression of your deepest self?

Here is another expression: "What do you do?" Almost always, people are referring to work when they say this. But is work really the most important thing we do in our lives? Suppose the expression referred to what kind of sacred path you follow? Imagine. You go to a party where you do not know many people but you hope to make new friends. Someone introduces himself and says, "What do you do?" Instead of saying "Software engineer," you answer, "I follow the Sun Cycles. My friends and I celebrate the Wheel of the Seasons. My favorite is the Autumn Equinox, when we make commitments to ourselves and leap over the fires. And this year we're building our own stone circle for the Summer Solstice in June. And you? What do you do?"

Instead of looking strangely at you, or hurrying away, your new acquaintance answers, "Mostly sacred dancing. Last week I went to a retreat and we followed the rhythms all the way back to the Great Mother. I also do Vision Quests. I love to go to a hilltop I know, where it's so silent I feel like I can see the whole world beneath me. My sister wants me to take her son there next week for his twelfth birthday."

Sound bizarre? All over the United States, there are people doing just these kinds of things. They may not be ready to share them with strangers at cocktail parties, but they are doing solo rituals in the woods or their apartments, dancing with ritual groups under the Full Moon, lighting fires in the dark of winter, chanting and meditating. They do this because they have found that ritual indeed gives their lives a deeper meaning than possessions or career.

Ritual reminds us that the world is a place of mystery, and that we ourselves are wondrous beings. Ritual celebrates physical reality—the seasons, the Sun and Moon and Stars, food, beauty, our bodies. At the same time, it opens us to unseen dimensions. The ritual revival, a genuine grassroots movement with groups and individuals all over the country, has sprung up in recent years precisely because people have hungered for such awareness.

In their search they have turned to those who know. In this case, that means the teachers, both alive and dead, of the great ritual traditions. And yet the purpose is never just academic. We do not seek just information, we seek experience. In this book we will look at examples and teachings from all over the world, from contemporary wise people and from anonymous artists and builders who lived thousands of years ago. We will look at these examples as inspirations rather than rules, for our goal is for you to develop your own rituals that give your life meaning. Though we will consider some of the rituals in detail, none of them are meant as scripts to follow blindly. They were created originally to express some special truth. In pursuit of that truth for yourself, it makes sense to adapt the rituals in any way meaningful for you.

The world is filled with religious traditions, mythologies, and sacred practices. All of them offer their own special wisdom. Where once people battled over who was right and who was wrong, now many of us recognize that all traditions have something to offer on the path to spirituality. Along with this recognition comes a desire to learn from many different sources. Teachers, too, understand this. The best rituals arise from this blend of ancient and modern traditions.

In the world of ritual today we find Zen Buddhist masters, mystical rabbis, Christian priests who embrace all the world's wisdom, African shamans, artists, healers, Taoist storytellers, and people who simply want to dance and sing with joy. The actual rituals themselves take the teachings out of the realm of theory and into physical and emotional reality.

Along with my friend and teaching partner, Mary K. Greer (a master ritualist in her own right), I have taught a yearly class at the Omega Institute for thirteen years. The class we teach concerns the wisdom coded into Tarot cards, those odd symbolic picture cards most people associate with fortune-telling. Over the centuries of its development the Tarot actually has evolved into a system of images meant to inspire people through the various stages of spiritual development. Mary and I use different techniques to help the symbolic ideas become real to people. We have everyone tell stories, we all visualize the cards in our minds and then imagine ourselves entering the pictures to talk to the characters, we ponder the

Hawk flying

meanings, we do readings for each other, we interpret dreams. . . . At the end of the week, all of this comes together in a ritual that takes up the entire morning.

This ritual begins playfully. A couple of days ahead of time, everyone picks a card without looking. The cards contain such figures as the Magician, the High Priestess, Justice, the Chariot driver, the Moon, and so on. On the final day, each person comes in costume as the card she or he received. We play a game of Guess the Character based on people's costumes and mini-performances everyone does as their card. Then we move into a more serious mood. In the center of the room an improvised altar on a velvet cloth holds objects symbolizing the four basic "Elements" of life—perhaps a candle for Fire, a chalice for Water, a feather for Air, and a stone for Earth, with a quartz crystal in the center for Spirit. Incense purifies the air. As each person silently enters the room, ritual leaders on either side of them perfume their bodies with incense and anoint them with aromatic oils diluted in water. The leaders whisper a blessing and a welcome to sacred space. Everyone takes their place in a circle.

The ritual continues with a visualization. Through deep rhythmic breathing, and then suggestions spoken by Mary and me, everyone takes a journey in her or his imagination. Vividly they see themselves climb a hill into brilliant light, where they dance with such freedom they can follow a hawk and fly over the mountains. When they come down, they enter the Spirit of the Tarot character whose costume they wear.

The heart of the ritual comes when each person speaks as her or his character. They do not do this in a self-conscious playacting kind of way, but as if they truly have become that figure. They give a message to the world and then to their normal selves. Through the years of doing this, I have seen some wondrous transformations. One man who had spent the entire week joking and making fun of himself became a Hermit who held up a light of truth to "Sam" and told him that he did not have to hide or be frightened anymore, that that part of his life was over. When he came out of the ritual, he knew it was true. One year a woman made a decision to join an Episcopal seminary, while another went home and enrolled in law school. The first is now an ordained priest who incorporates Pagan goddess worship in her Christian rituals. The second fights for women's rights out of a law practice.

Such changes become possible because ritual involves our whole being. We use our knowledge, our imaginations, our emotions, our sense of wonder and mystery. Through this intensity we come to know ourselves and our own truths more deeply than we would have thought possible. As we travel through this book I invite you to discover the wonders in the world of ritual—and in yourself.

One

❖

The World
of Ritual

The Many Sides of Ritual

You stand in a circle with your friends and family at the end of the longest day of the year. From today until December 21, half a year away, the days will get shorter and shorter. You and the others have joined to celebrate this peak moment of light. A wreath of flowers adorns your head; your daughter made it for you. Woven strands of flowers and ribbons of all colors drape the trees, a sight that thrills you with its vibrant beauty. To one side stand picnic tables filled with food and wildflowers. On another side men and women, dressed all in white, hold torches, ready to light the huge bonfire.

What a wonderful day, you think, filled with joy and love, with play and moments of intense emotion, with the closeness and love that come when people join together to celebrate their lives and their union with nature.

As the Sun reaches the horizon line, a song begins, written by the woman who invited you to the ritual. Very simple, it thanks the light as it begins its long journey to the darkness of Winter. The song rises in intensity until, as the last arc of the Sun dips out of sight, everyone lifts their arms and shouts. At that same instant, the bonfire leaps to life. You and your daughter hold hands and begin to dance, laughing, your hearts full of love.

Ritual is about connections and openings. It connects us to each other, to nature, to the cycles and rhythms of life. It opens our hearts to love and to intense emotion—sadness and longing as well as joy. And it opens a space for what we call the sacred, or spirituality, to enter our lives.

Before we explore all the details of ritual, the how-to and the great ritual traditions, let's take a moment to discover how ritual already appears in our lives, even when we do not identify it.

Special Moments

Are there special times and moments in your life, or special actions that touch a place deep inside you? Maybe you put your child to bed each night in a particular way. The two of you say a blessing together, or you ask your child what happened that day, or the two of you describe something that makes you feel grateful. Then you give the child his teddy bear, tuck him in with a kiss on the forehead, or maybe say a little poem that brings a smile. You do it the same way every night, partly because if you forget something your child will tell you to do it "right," and partly because you remember the things your own mother or father did, and how those nightly repetitions made you feel secure and loved as you fell asleep.

The things we do with our families often feature a repetition that gives them more meaning each time we do them. They do not need to be nightly. You wake up each year on your birthday to the smell of pancakes on the grill. As you lie in bed you know that in a minute your children will walk in with the tray holding the apple pancakes and maple syrup, the cut-up grapefruit, the two chocolate truffles on their little silver dish, and the single rose in a champagne glass (because that first time he did it, your husband couldn't find a vase the right size).

Every Valentine's Day you and your partner go to that bed-and-breakfast you discovered when you were first dating. You make sure to get the same room and go to the same restaurant overlooking the lake. When you return to your room you put on the portable CD player so you can dance to the same song you heard on the radio that first Valentine's Day you came here. The room, the restaurant, the song—they all help you rediscover the wonder of first love, and realize how much that love has deepened year after year.

Ritual helps us acknowledge the important moments in our lives. By doing things the same way, we recognize the patterns and continuity of our lives, while at the same time we place those moments outside of the ordinary flow of events.

When repetition occurs in everyday activities without thought or feeling, it may become boring. Jobs that require you to do the same task over and over can numb your senses and make life itself seem dreary. But when we find some meaningful activity and repeat it in a context of emotion, the repetition can lift us out of that same dreariness.

Such activities are rituals, not just because we always do them the same way, or

Do We Have to Believe in Spirits?

In much of this book we will be looking at rituals that invoke various "Spirits." Sometimes we will call these figures gods or goddesses, sometimes we will use names from different religious traditions. We will refer to the ideas and images of Christianity and Buddhism and Native American religion. We will talk about "messages" they give us, even "conversations" we might have with such "beings" as Grandmother Moon. And we will offer them blessings and thank them for their help.

Do we need to actually believe in all these "Radiant Ones" (to use a favorite term of my own) in order to do rituals, or even just read this book?

In my own quarter century of working with rituals I have found that they work best when we find our own comfort level of belief. Thus, you can view the Spirits simply as creations of the human mind. Or you look at them as true independent beings. Or you may fall somewhere in the middle. All the points of view are valid, all contribute to the beauty and meaning of the ritual.

even because they remind us of love and what really matters in life. They are rituals because they create moments outside the ordinary flow of events. We can call such moments time out of time. The break from our ordinary lives heightens our senses and reminds us of who we are. When such time out of time goes beyond the simple pleasures of quiet moments or annual celebrations to open us to spiritual awareness, then we move to the larger world of sacred ritual.

Secular Rituals

In American life today, most of us know the pleasures and renewal of ritual primarily in secular settings. For example, *Monday Night Football.* Fans increase their enjoyment by always doing it the same way—the same seat on the couch, the same beer and chips. The raw physicality and strong emotion of the game provide an expression of victory and defeat usually uncommon in a society where most of our battles are won and lost in the office. These weekly rituals culminate in the national celebration of Super Bowl Sunday. The parties for this television event have long eclipsed the football game itself. People begin planning as early as November. Already there are ritual foods, such as giant sandwiches.

Other traditional secular rituals in America are Thanksgiving and July Fourth. Once again, we recognize the qualities of ritual. Everyone watches fireworks on the Fourth. And on Thanksgiving, people eat the same foods all over the country: turkey with dressing, cranberry sauce, and pumpkin pie.

Thanksgiving actually derives from the much older tradition of harvest festivals. In ancient Israel, for example, the major holidays were all linked to the harvesting of specific crops that ripened at different times of the year. In ancient times, people were at nature's mercy. So much could go wrong that people felt a need to give thanks once the food was safely harvested. They addressed their gratitude to God or the gods who made life possible.

In modern Western culture, most of us have never faced the possibility of a serious food shortage. We may worry about having enough money to buy food, but the food itself is always available for purchase. This is very different from a famine, where the food simply does not exist. And yet we still feel that powerful need to give thanks. And so we extend our gratitude to the less tangible elements of our lives, such as family, love, fulfilling work, the beauty of nature. And once again, many people make this actual thanks-giving a ritual part of the November meal, with each person having a chance to express their own gratitude.

Religious rituals involve the retelling of the sacred stories, such as the manger birth for Christmas, or the Jewish liberation from Egypt for Passover. So, too, secular rituals such as Thanksgiving and July Fourth involve stories, the Pilgrims' search for religious freedom, and the heroic deprivations of Washington's army at Valley Forge. These national myths bind us together as a people.

Layers of Ritual

Ritual often has a multilayered, or nested, quality, involving the individual, the family, and the larger community. In his book *Ritual: Power, Healing, and Community,* Malidoma Patrice Somé, a teacher who bridges the gap between African and Western experience, describes the layers of ritual in his own Dagara culture.

In Dagara society, all adult members of the village attend communal rituals. These mass ceremonies, where everyone plays a specific part, provide a setting that allows family rituals to take place and be effective. And this in turn creates the space for people's individual rituals. It works the other way as well. If an individual does not perform the rituals required of him or her, this weakens the family, and in turn the entire community's connection to the gods. This happens because in Dagara life people are not isolated individuals whose lives are meaningful only to themselves. Instead, everyone belongs to the community and the Spirits. If someone does not fulfill his or her spiritual obligation, it weakens the spiritual web for everyone. But when everyone does do his or her part this web becomes amazingly strong and a support for each person.

In modern cultures, where the primary cultural rituals are secular (even Christmas has lost most of its specific religious meaning), people have begun to re-create rituals from the bottom up. They draw on their own creativity and expe-

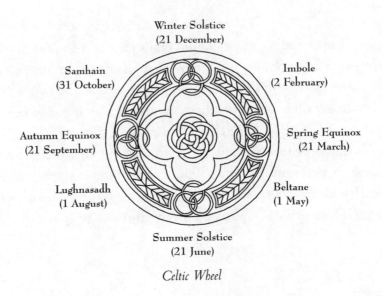

Winter Solstice
(21 December)

Samhain
(31 October)

Imbole
(2 February)

Autumn Equinox
(21 September)

Spring Equinox
(21 March)

Lughnasadh
(1 August)

Beltane
(1 May)

Summer Solstice
(21 June)

Celtic Wheel

riences to restore spiritual meaning to their lives. These modern ceremonies, however, often draw upon ancient traditions. We may make medicine bags, inspired by the healing rituals of American Indians. Or we may follow the Celtic Wheel of the Year, with its eight seasonal rituals.

Teachers such as Michael Harner, founder of the School of Shamanic Studies, bring the varied experiences of the world's shamans to modern spiritual seekers. "Shaman" is a word from the Tungus people of Siberia to describe the tribal healer. From Siberia to North America to prehistoric Europe to ancient Japan to Africa and elsewhere, the people we call shamans have traveled in their visions to the mythical World of the Gods to bring back healing and wisdom. Through drumming, trance work, and ancient images, in his workshops at Omega, Harner teaches people from our secular techno-culture to reawaken mysteries that our ancestors once knew intimately.

As we begin to rediscover the power of ritual, we also increase our sense of community. We come together in groups to share our rituals and to give them more power, for when we do such things with others the result is often much more than the sum of its parts. And slowly the group rituals begin to affect the wider society, resulting in a greater overall awareness of the sacred.

When we celebrate a ritual, whether sacred or secular, we gain strength knowing that everyone does it in a similar way. Thanksgiving holds such power-

A Modern Communal Ritual

An example of a contemporary ritual that has gained wide acceptance (it even appears now on business calendars, along with Christmas and Chanukah) is the holiday of Kwanzaa. This seven-day series of rituals between Christmas and New Year's began as the brainchild of an African-American academic, Maulana Karenga, who borrowed elements of African traditions, harvest festivals, and Chanukah (a candle for each day) to create a holiday that would honor both African history and virtues vital to individual growth and a healthy community. Against the skepticism of many, who believed that no one could deliberately create a mass ritual, Kwanzaa has taken its place as a major Winter Solstice event.

ful meaning for us because we know that all across the country people are doing the same thing. At the same time, each family produces its own variations to make the day its own—a particular pie, or a special way to honor grandparents. If everyone did it *exactly* the same, it would become simply ritualistic, like a prayer that has lost its meaning. True ritual acknowledges personal as well as communal experience.

Kwanzaa candles

Kwanzaa ears of corn

The Secular and the Sacred

However much secular rituals fulfill our desire for celebration and community, they lack the extra dimension found in sacred ceremonies. They may give us moments out of ordinary time, but they do not show us glimpses of a world beyond our ordinary experience. They do not address our yearning to touch the divine and let it enter our lives.

There are two components to sacred ritual. The first is common to secular rituals as well: a set action or pattern of actions. Usually these actions serve a purpose, such as healing sickness, honoring rites of passage (for example, wedding vows), channeling grief (funerals), recognizing the rhythms of nature, or giving thanks. The second separates sacred ritual from secular: We invite divine power to enter our lives for the period of time the ritual takes place. We can think of sacred ritual as the intersection of ordinary reality and spiritual reality. Ritual provides a safe framework, or container, for us to experience the sacred.

Without this protection we risk overwhelming ourselves. In the 1960s and '70s many people experimented with direct experiences of the sacred. Many took hallucinogenic drugs. Some of these, such as mushrooms, had been used by people in indigenous cultures for many centuries to carry them to the "Otherworld" of the gods. For many in the '60s and '70s, these experiments resulted in genuine awareness of spiritual dimensions. For others, however, the lack of any context induced excitement, but also delusions and fear. Traditional cultures use such substances only with special training and guides.

Ritual and Traditional Religion

Ritual, with its opening to spiritual truth, is a basic human need. Many people leave behind the religious training they received as children because they simply find it too empty—prayers and actions repeated over and over without a thought to any meaning or connection to people's lives. A container without content. And yet if you ask them what they recall fondly, it often turns out to be some aspect of ritual. A church filled with flowers for Easter. A choir singing "Gloria In Excelsis Deo" on Christmas Eve. The piercing sound of the shofar (ram's horn) at the end of Rosh Hashanah, the Jewish New Year. Because of such memories, many people discover themselves returning to their family religion, but doing so in a church or a movement that restores meaning and mystery to the container of religion.

Often this restoration involves the creation of new rituals based on old ones. For example, traditional Judaism includes a monthly recognition of the New Moon, called Rosh Chodesh. Many Jewish women have formed small groups to perform monthly rituals that explore women's lives and involvement in Judaism. Matthew Fox, a Christian priest and philosopher, has created a "Techno Cosmic Mass" as part of the renewal of Christian tradition in what he calls "Creation Spirituality."

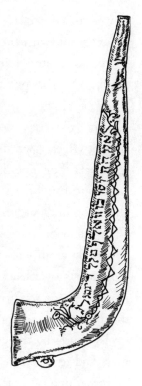

Shofar

Ritual and Myth

Ritual often involves stories. The stories educate us about our Spirits and gods. In Christianity, the Gospels tell the story of Jesus' life, death, and resurrection. In some rituals initiates take on the experiences of the gods by symbolically acting out key moments in a myth. The traditional Christian mass repeats the experience of the disciples at Jesus' "Last Supper."

One of the world's most elaborate rituals took place in ancient Greece. Called the Greater Mysteries, it was based on a myth about how the god of death kidnapped Persephone, daughter of the grain goddess, Demeter. In her grief, Demeter stopped all the plants from growing until the gods forced Death to restore Persephone to life. In the ritual, the thousands of participants, men as well as women, took the part of Demeter (a Roman coin shows the face of the emperor, with the title "goddess" because he had been initiated at Eleusis). They sat on stools and drank a barley drink like the one Demeter supposedly drank. On the pivotal fifth night, they all ran with torches in search of Persephone.

The Mysteries took place every five years for over two thousand years in the ancient Greek town of Eleusis, outside Athens. As many as five thousand people took part. For nine days, beginning with a daylong parade along the coast from Athens to bring the sacred ritual objects to the temples, and ending with a secret revelation underground, all the participants did the same things at the same time. They even wore the same clothes, shrouds that they tore up after the ritual to make swaddling clothes for babies.

Experts on Eleusis, like the Jungian scholar Karl Kerenyi, have described the Mysteries as a way for the participants to overcome the fear of death. They did this through taking on the roles of the main characters of the story.

By imitating the gods, people join with them. They transcend their ordinary lives, and for the brief period of the ritual, that time out of time, they feel part of something larger than themselves. Such eloquent witnesses as the Greek dramatist Sophocles and the Roman statesman Cicero testified to the power of the Eleusinian Mysteries.

Ritual As Performance

The Greater Mysteries were a spiritual event on a grand scale. Not every ritual aspires to such heights. We may do rituals simply to mark a transition in our lives, or to express our closeness to nature, or simply to step out of the rush of our hectic lives. We may do rituals for practical purposes—to help us overcome an eating problem, or to enter into a new job or a new relationship. Whatever the purpose, rituals usually involve some level of performance. We do not just state our intentions or beliefs. We act them out in some way. We may wear ritual clothes, or hold symbolic objects, or write something on a piece of paper and then burn it in a

The Many Moods of Ritual

Ritual is not just solemn or grand. Ritual expresses the whole range of human emotion and experience.

Here are just some of the possibilities:

Transformation—rituals can help us break down old patterns that no longer serve us. They can release us to new ways of dealing with life. For example, people with eating disorders may perform a ritual about food to free themselves to eat In a more healthful way.

Celebration—how long has it been since you last danced with abandon to a great rhythm? Probably you did this at a concert or disco. Imagine releasing your raw energy in a sacred setting. Massive street parties, like the Carneval in Brazil, derive directly from ancient rituals (see chapter 5). You don't need to go to Brazil for this. You can create a ritual where you dance, sing with all your might, or just shout for joy.

Mourning—modern funerals seem designed to rush people through their grief as quickly as possible. "It's time to get on with your life," we tell people as soon as the body is in the ground. Older cultures knew better. They designed rituals that allow people to fully enter the pain of loss. Only then can healing come.

Rest—how often do you really allow yourself to relax? How often do you set time aside just to do nothing, with no guilt about that long list of responsibilities? Using ritual to give yourself the gift of true rest can return you to the world refreshed, with new insights.

Our journey in ritual has begun. We have seen some of the forms of ritual as well as some of the ways ritual can give our lives more meaning. We have looked at the difference between sacred and secular rituals and the way we all have experienced secular rituals such as Thanksgiving. At the same time there is a further dimension to sacred rituals that gives them a special power, including the ability to move us in very deep ways. In the next chapter we will look at what makes a ritual a spiritual experience.

bonfire, or drink wine that we have previously blessed for the ceremony. Ritual is not just theory. It's action.

RESOURCES

BOOKS

Feinstein, David, Ph.D., Introduction by Jean Houston. *The Mythic Path.* New York: Putnam, 1997.

Fox, Matthew. *Original Blessing.* Santa Fe, N. Mex.: Bear & Co., 1996.

Harner, Michael. *The Way of the Shaman.* San Francisco: HarperSanFrancisco, 1991.

Houston, Jean. *A Passion for the Possible.* San Francisco: HarperSanFrancisco, 1998.

Kerenyi, Karl. *Eleusis: Archetypal Image of Mother and Daughter.* Princeton, N.J.: Princeton University Press, 1991 (pb).

O'Donohue, John. *Anam Cara: A Book of Celtic Wisdom.* New York: HarperCollins, 1997.

Riley, Dorothy Winbush. *The Complete Kwanzaa, Reprint edition.* New York: HarperPerennial, 1996.

Somé, Malidoma Patrice. *Ritual.* New York: Penguin, 1993.

WEB SITES

For Jean Houston's Mystery School, see www.jeanhouston.org.

For Matthew Fox's Graduate Studies in Creation Spirituality, see www.creationspirituality.com.

For Michael Harner and the Foundation for Shamanic Studies, see www.shamanism.org.

2.

Embodying
the Sacred

We have seen how rituals gain extra dimension when they open us to "sacred" awareness. What does this really mean? In this chapter, we will turn to the teachers of the great spiritual traditions who have gone before us and who can help show us the way. Some of these teachers died thousands of years ago; others are alive today.

What Is Spirituality?

Stop a moment and think about this question. What does spirituality mean to you? Is it being a good person? Is it living your life according to a set of principles, maybe those of your religion or the Golden Rule plus the Ten Commandments? Is it self-sacrifice? Is it charity toward the less fortunate?

These are all moral ideas. Important as morality is, spirituality encompasses more: the sacred, what we might define as an opening to a power beyond ordinary reality. Without a connection to the sacred, morality can become little more than duty and self-denial. By contrast, when we sense that awesome power of the sacred, acting with love becomes a joy rather than a duty. Just as we need to do good deeds to make real the moral teachings of religion, so we need to embody the sacred in ritual to give it reality.

So what does "sacred" mean? Is it simply whatever is written down in the Bible? Is it the sum of the Bible plus all the other famous religious texts, such as the Muslim Koran, the Hindu Bhagavad-Gita, the Taoist *Tao Te Ching*? Is it the teachings of living gurus and other inspired leaders? Is it some magic power they possess? Is it some magic power in certain objects, like the Cross, or candles blessed by a priest? Is it a magic power found in special places, such as Stonehenge, or the Old City in Jerusalem?

Something in Ourselves

Or is the "magic" something we experience in ourselves? Do we know the sacred more by the experience than by any definition? Maybe we can define this complex term as a divine presence that we understand directly in our lives. The sense of awe

Ecstasy

and wonder that fills us—that tingling all over the body, the hairs standing up. The desire to laugh, or cry out, or maybe weep, not from sadness or even joy, but just from so much amazement, and love, filling our small selves.

Whirling dervish

In its most extreme form we call this feeling "ecstasy," a Greek word that means to stand outside yourself—in other words, an excitement or joy that transports you beyond your normal sense of who you are. You lose your limitations, your weariness, your isolation, and instead discover a oneness with the world around you.

We find examples of ecstasy in every religious tradition, from the trance states brought on by hours of drumming and dancing in Africa to the intense meditations of Tibetan Buddhism. Christian mystics, such as St. John of the Cross and St. Theresa of Avila, described the flood of joy that overwhelmed them as they meditated on Christ. The image of Christ on the cross is actually one of pain, and yet Christians refer to the crucifixion as "the Passion," and when they join with it the feeling is one of love. The Persian mystic Rumi wrote of God as "the Beloved." The eighteenth-century Jewish teacher Israel ben Eliezer, known as the Baal Shem Tov (Master of the Good Name), began the movement of Hasidism, in which dances and ecstatic singing (often without words) lead to knowledge of God.

Pir Vilayat Khan, Sufi master and author of *Eyes of God* (among others), describes ecstasy as "intoxication." According to Khan, the Sufis, an ancient order of spiritual seekers, are drunk all the time, on the wine of God. God is not a mysterious being far away, but a direct experience of divine love.

Pir Vilayat Khan writes that Spirit "transfuses" matter. Since our cells come from the cells of our parents, and all the way back through evolution, we actually contain the cells of all our ancestors, not just humans, but the plants, the fish, even the rocks. This is not a poetic metaphor but a scientific fact. Actually, since our solar system coalesced from the remains of long-dead stars, we can say that we are all made out of stardust.

What does all this mean? Khan writes that we all are part of a greater reality, all of us connected to everything else.

The Sufi, he says, understands something even further. We carry in our bodies not just the physical inheritance of our ancestors, going back to the first humans and beyond. We also carry—in our bodies, in our cells—qualities of all "higher beings," the angels, *djinns* (an Islamic term for Earth Spirits), archangels, "right up to the top," as Khan puts it. God is literally in our bodies. We deny this because to accept it would overwhelm our narrow view of what is possible. Because this truth is so powerful, we hide from it behind our belief that we are alone and isolated.

Do you feel the intoxication of simply reading about such things? Imagine, then, the "drunkenness" of the Sufi, or anyone else from the world's myriad spiritual paths, who actually experiences it.

The Sacred Beyond Us

Is the sacred, then, just something we experience in our bodies? The answer from all these traditions is a resounding No. The feeling we have that we are alone inside our bodies, isolated from the rest of existence, is an illusion. This illusion is what makes us tired, or depressed, or lonely, or afraid. When we break the illusion open we discover unlimited sources of energy and belief. And yet there is a paradox here. The way we get beyond our feeling of being isolated in our bodies is through the physical acts of ritual.

Rituals do not automatically produce ecstatic or trance experiences. Nor do we want them to. One important discovery of the modern ritual revival is that we do rituals for all sorts of purposes, from healing to prosperity to celebration of a new love. And yet within all rituals lies that desire to make the sacred a reality in our daily lives.

A Ritual for Letting Go

All these paradoxes may remind some people of the *Tao Te Ching,* the ancient Chinese evocation of the Tao, usually translated as "the Way." Lao Tzu, the author of the *Tao Te Ching,* tells us that we can find the divine only by not seeking it. Harmony with life comes only when we do nothing to achieve it.

For many people, especially in the West, this is maddening. You want to experience sacred oneness, and here comes Lao Tzu to tell you that the only way you can get it is by not wanting it. But you *do* want it. Should you pretend you don't want it? No, the wise tell us, that's even worse.

One way through this confusion is ritual. Here is a ceremony for a small group of people. I call it Letting Go of God. Everyone brings their favorite sacred images—prayer books, amulets, small statues, shawls, T-shirts of goddesses, beads, stones, a paper where you have written the names of gods and goddesses—whatever symbolizes your desire to know God. If you can wear it, do so (though unless you really trust the other people, you might want to wear something under it). In the center of the room place a large empty bowl or cauldron.

Everyone stands around the cauldron and holds hands. Since the ritual involves a visualization, someone should volunteer ahead of time to act as leader. This is not a role of power but in fact of surrender, for the "leader" must sense the energy of the group and flow with it, gently giving it shape rather than directing it. Usually, this will mean someone experienced in ritual and meditation.

Begin by closing your eyes and breathing deeply. As your breathing becomes more relaxed, feel it merge with the others so that a group breath takes shape. Feel the rhythm of it. When the leader senses the moment has come, she or he will begin the visualization.

A "visualization" means simply a spoken description that allows people to vividly imagine themselves in some situation.

The leader will tell the group to imagine themselves in a wonderful place outdoors, with a warm Sun, flowing water, flowering trees, and a gentle breeze. You are there with a box full of your dearest treasures, the divine symbols that matter most to you in the world. Now you listen to the sound of the water and begin to follow it upstream. You become aware of a mountain nearby, and at the top of it a glorious light, so radiant it outshines the Sun. You pick up your box of treasures and begin to climb. When you get to the top you will display all your sacred possessions.

But the way is hard, and you know that to continue you must give something up. Take one of your special objects and place it in the cauldron. Now you imagine going on, lightened and energized. After a time you feel the weight once more, and the heat, for, after all, the light is very intense. If you have worn some piece of sacred clothing, take it off and place it in the cauldron.

Do this twice more, and the last time surrender the remainder of your divine possessions. Each time feel how much lighter you become.

Now free, you dance your way to the top, where you discover no ball of fire, but only a pure light and sweet fresh air. Whoever wishes may actually dance or move about. When the leader senses that the group has touched a point of peace, everyone moves to the center. Eyes closed, put your hands in the cauldron. Feel the streams of memory and devotion in the collected emblems of the sacred. By letting go you all share each other's power and belief, even each other's experience. At the end, each person may take back or give away whatever they wish.

Taking Part in the World Around Us

An old saying tells us that we are not humans having spiritual experiences, but Spirits having human experiences. Whatever we believe about the existence of a soul or an afterlife, the fact remains that in this life we exist in bodies. We take part in the world around us. Ritual can help us connect our physical life with our spiritual one. If we do a ritual to bless our food, we learn to recognize the miracle of life in everything we eat. We will no longer eat unconsciously, but instead with amazement that we can take parts of other creatures directly into our bodies. If we do a ritual to heal, then each time we follow a medical procedure we will take in the awe that the body can restore itself.

Body and Soul

Medicine bag

Many people believe that the body and the soul, the material world and spiritual truth, are somehow opposites. In ritual we discover that the two go together. They strengthen each other. For example, an American Indian medicine bundle is a group of things that may seem meaningless to an outsider—a feather, say, or tobacco, or a bear claw. The person who makes it, however, understands the meaning of each object. Your own medicine bundle might include a shell you found on a beach. My own pouch contains a small quartz rock a friend gave me during a ritual years ago. Individually the things in a medicine bundle possess power because they have meaning for you. Together they give strength to each other so that the bundle becomes your opening to the sacred.

Ritual opens a doorway in the invisible wall that seems to separate the spiritual and the physical. The formal quality of ritual allows us to move into the space between the worlds, experience what we need, and then step back and once more close the doorway so we can return to our lives enriched.

Your Own Practice

You do not actually have to accept the ideas of any single tradition, or even believe in divine forces at all, to take part in ritual. Ritual is a direct experience, not a doctrine. Though it will certainly help to suspend your disbelief for the time of the ritual, you could attend a group ritual, take part in the chanting and drumming, and find yourself transported to a sense of wonder at the simple beauty of it all without ever actually believing in any of the claims made or the Spirits invoked.

You can also adapt rituals to your own beliefs. If evolution means more to you than a Creator, you could see ritual as a way to connect yourself to the life force.

We spoke of ritual for different purposes, such as healing or love. The idea that the right ritual might magically cure someone who is sick or lonely might seem like superstition. We often hear of people who refuse medical treatment because it is against their religion. Or a friend might tell us of a storefront "Reader and Advisor" who promises to light a special candle or perform a spell to bring a partner into your life. Ritual does not replace action, but it can support the practical things we do to address our problems.

Ritual allows divine life energy to charge our actions. It casts a model for what we hope to happen. If you do a ritual before surgery, you are inviting the Spirits to support you. If nothing else, you create a positive attitude in yourself.

Where Do Babies Come From?

In his book *The Way of the Animal Powers*, the great mythologist Joseph Campbell described the process of making a baby for the Gunwinngu people of northern Australia. When a man and woman wanted to have a child they would have sex and then the man would do a ritual before a painting of "child germs," round heads with dark mysterious eyes and no mouths. These paintings represent the eternal spirits of the ancestors. After the ritual, the man would dream first of finding one of the images, then, in a second dream, of projecting it into his wife. The dream would invite the ancestral spirit to enter the woman's womb so that a baby might grow there.

If an anthropologist asked the Gunwinngu "Where do babies come from?" the tribe might very well answer "The paintings of the ancestors" and describe the ritual. We can imagine such an anthropologist writing in his field notes "The primitive tribe does not know that babies come from sex." But of course they do. They just know something else as well, that babies—people—are spirit as well as body, and they are inviting this positive energy to be present through their ritual. Maybe we are the ones who are naive in our belief that intercourse is all you need to create a living being. Haven't all of us heard stories of couples trying to have a baby, timing the exact day and hour to make love, and still failing, only to succeed when they stopped being so scientific? Maybe all they needed was the right ritual.

Omens—Watching the World's Response

Ritual activity joins together the spiritual and the physical. While this happens primarily during the ritual, sometimes the world seems to respond in subtle ways, as if to acknowledge and support what we are doing. You may pick up a magazine and open it to a picture of Botticelli's painting of the goddess Venus on the same day you are planning a love ritual. If a number figures in your ritual—the number 5, say, for the Wiccan pentagram, or 22, sacred in Jewish mysticism—you might find you encounter the number with amazing frequency.

One afternoon, while working on this book at my local library, I wrote about a Sufi ritual in which people chant, over and over, the Sufi Muslim prayer "La illha illa llah hu"—"There is no God save God." Though the words looked beautiful on paper, I had never heard them sung. I finished my work and went to my car, where I turned on the NPR program "All Things Considered." Immediately I heard soft lilting voices chanting "La illha illa llah hu." The announcer then came on to say that this prayer came from a new CD called *Sufi Soul Music.*

We can call such experiences "omens." They are not good and certainly not bad. Instead, we can take them as acknowledgment. We have reached out to the spiritual dimension, and now that "unseen world" is allowing us to glimpse its presence, as if to say "Yes, we recognize your efforts."

We should not expect omens every time we do a ritual. If we look for them and do not find them, that does not mean the ritual did not work. Rituals aren't magic tricks. We do them to change ourselves more than to change the world. When omens do happen, however, we can enjoy them with that special thrill of recognition.

The psychologist Carl Jung and Wolfgang Pauli, a physicist, invented the term "synchronicity" to describe what Jung called "meaningful coincidences."

"Beauty is truth, truth beauty."

Ritual rekindles our wonder at life. It reminds us of the beauty of the world in all its stunning variety. The great Romantic poet John Keats wrote, "Beauty is truth, truth beauty / That is all ye know on earth, and all ye need to know." Keats and the other writers and artists of his time were seeking alternatives to religion, which for them had lost its power to inspire. Some Romantics, such as Wordsworth, found their alternative in nature. Keats looked for it in art. For both, appreciation of beauty led to what the Romantics called "the sublime," or what we call "the sacred." Some people indeed can touch this exalted state simply through contemplation of a sunset or a Grecian urn. Most, however, need a more active involvement to awaken to ecstasy. Because ritual directly uses our senses, it can involve us in the beauty that leads to truth.

The beauty of ritual energizes all our senses—the smell of incense; the taste of wine or fruit, or a cake baked in the shape of your favorite goddess; the touch of your own medicine bag or the velvet you use to lay out your altar; the music of your own voice as you chant, the memories and emotions we share in a group, the sounds of the ocean laced with the low whistles of whales; the light of a fire on the longest night of the year. All these, with the costumes we wear, the wild movements, the words of power we call out, they become our own journey to the sublime. As Pir Vilayat Khan writes, "It's deadly to live without beauty. It's unbearable."

People who do spiritual work will very often report of some synchronicity just when they need it. Here is an example even more explicit than my discovery of Sufi soul music. Merlin Stone, author of *When God Was a Woman* (a founding text of the goddess movement), once described how she could not find a vital book she needed for her research. She had tried antiquarian booksellers, libraries, all without success. One afternoon she went to the supermarket and saw an old book on the floor in one of the aisles. When she picked it up it was the exact work she needed.

Meaningful coincidences are usually just like that, a small boost at the moment we need it. The Spirit world will not solve our problems or do our work for us. But it will, to use an old expression, help us if we help ourselves.

A World of Many Traditions

Unlike our ancestors, many of us draw our beliefs from more than one tradition. The world has become much more open than ever before. Pioneering anthropologists and archaeologists revealed the magnificent variety of human spiritual expression. Television allows us to see the ways of people on the far side of the Earth, fulfilling the philosopher Marshall McLuhan's famous prophecy of a "global village." The Internet allows us to gather information and discover new ideas simply by following a series of links on the world wide web.

Even if we choose to follow only one path, we still can learn from others. Even teachers of a particular path may have studied others. The Christian or Jewish masters who are reviving their own ritual traditions, such as Matthew Fox or Rabbi David Cooper, probably have studied the methods and ideas of yoga, or Tibetan Buddhism.

Many people in the West have looked to tribal and indigenous cultures as models for ritual and a living relationship to nature. At the same time, many tribal traditions long ago absorbed ideas from the world religions. Christianity and Islam have greatly influenced the African religions, which still keep their own powerful truths and intense rituals. This is even more true in the Americas, where the slaveholders attempted to impose Christianity to wipe out African people's cultural identity. Instead, the Africans managed to adapt Christianity for their own purposes. In Haiti, for example, the African gods sometimes took the names of Christian saints. Today, many people not of African descent have sought initiation in such African-American traditions as Vodou (Haiti), Santeria (Mexico), and Candomblé (Brazil). One thing that draws them to these practices is the intense use of ritual. In the world of ritual we all share the wonder and mystery of sacred experience.

Ritual in the World's Religions

All of the world's religious traditions have rich ritual traditions from which we can learn. This does not mean we have to believe in their gods or their teachings. It does not even mean we have to follow the rituals word for word, gesture for gesture. Instead, we can evaluate the traditions and adapt them, with proper respect, to our own needs.

We already have looked at some of the ideas of Sufism and African (Dagara) rituals. Following is a very brief sampling from other great ritual traditions.

Christianity

Traditional Christianity sees Jesus as God in the form of a human being. Though pure himself, Jesus accepted all of humanity's collective burdens and allowed himself to be sacrificed on the cross. He was raised three days later to prove he had overcome sin as well as death. In a sense, then, Christianity is built on a grand ritual, the death and resurrection of a perfect being.

In almost all of the many Christian denominations, acceptance of Jesus comes through the rite of baptism. The Gospels tell us that Jesus himself was baptized by John the Baptist. Whether done as an infant or a grown person, baptism washes away the person's sins and marks a spiritual rebirth. Some people receive new, or baptismal, names.

Orthodox Christianity and Catholicism are dense with ritual, perhaps the most important of which is the Mass. Jesus and his followers were all Jews. The Gospels of Matthew, Mark, and Luke tell us that when Jesus knew his death was imminent, he celebrated with his disciples a ritual meal that biblical scholars generally believe was something akin to the Jewish Passover seder (see chapter 5), which involves unleavened bread and wine. (The Gospel According to John places the so-called Last Supper a day before Passover, perhaps to signify that Jesus' execution the next day was the symbolic sacrificial lamb that the Jews slaughtered for their Passover meals.) In the Gospel According to Mark we read: "While they were eating, he took a loaf of bread, and after blessing it he broke it, gave it to them, and said, 'Take; this is my body.' Then he took a cup, and after giving thanks he gave it to them, and all of them drank from it. He said to them, 'This is my blood of the covenant, which is poured out for many' " (Mark 14:22–24). Today, what is

Water and Ritual

We do not need to take on Christian beliefs to understand the ritual power of immersion in water. In fact, we find this same idea all over the world, such as the Hindu practice of bathing in the Ganges River to cleanse the soul. Water washes us clean. It liberates us from the past. You could use immersion as part of a ritual after divorce or some other life-changing transition. Rituals with water also help us if we have passed through some great danger, either physical or emotional.

You can do a ritual with water in your own shower or bath. You might, however, want to find a place in nature (weather permitting), such as a stream or river. It should be isolated enough that you can do your ritual without fear of embarrassment. Prepare ahead of time. This means thinking about what you want to say, what situations you want to release from your life. Consider taking ritual objects, something that represents the past, and something to symbolize your hopes for the future.

On the day of the ritual, wear old clothes. Bring a fresh set with you. Wear a bathing suit if you are outside. Invoke whatever Spirits or gods you wish to help you (see chapter 10 for instructions on a general pattern for personal rituals). Hold up your representation of the past. Speak about your experience, what you have learned as well as what you want to leave behind. Set it behind you. Take off the old clothes and put them behind you as well.

Now ask the water to cleanse and release you. Hold up the symbol of the future and speak of what you want to create in your life. Set it down before you. Step into the water with the image of your hopes clearly in your mind. Take a deep breath and immerse yourself completely. Stay under for a few seconds and then rise. Step out of the water, dry yourself, and dress in your new clothes. As you dress, see yourself beginning the new phase of your life. Thank the water and whatever gods or Spirits you have invoked. When you pack up your things, put the old clothes and the symbol of the past in a separate bag. You might want to donate the old clothes to charity.

also known as the eucharist (which is Greek for the Hebrew word that means "blessing") is a ritual that commemorates the death and resurrection of Jesus much like the events of the Exodus are recalled during the Jewish celebration of the Passover.

Many modern Christians have felt a need to recast both the ideas and practices of their two-thousand-year-old religion. One of the leaders in this movement is Matthew Fox, whose autobiography describes him as a "post-denominational priest." Fox was ordained as a priest in 1967. Over time he developed his concept of Creation Spirituality. This doctrine involves a celebration of the world in all its wonder. It also borrows ideas and teachings from Eastern and indigenous religions. And it rejects such traditional Christian ideas as original sin. Fox's most well-known book is titled *Original Blessing*. The world and humanity are sacred.

Buddhism

Buddhism has experienced a great increase in popularity in the United States over the past thirty years. Americans seem to find in Buddhism a contemplative and practical aspect they have not been able to find in other spiritual traditions. Its rituals, as well as its meditation component, inspire a sense of inner peace that the religious traditions they grew up with—most likely Christianity or Judaism—have not offered them. In Buddhism, one learns how to seek this sense of equanimity not just in the meditation hall but in everything they do in their daily lives. Some would hardly call it a religion because the Buddha, its founder, rejected the notion of any devotional reverence toward anything but the truth about existence and the phenomenal world—a truth to which each individual must come to on his or her own through many years of practice.

The word "Buddha" is not a personal name. It's a Sanskrit word that means "enlightened being," one who has achieved liberation from the cycles of life, death, and rebirth. The historical Buddha lived in the sixth century B.C.E. This Buddha was a prince in what is now northern India. His name was Siddhartha. The story goes that he left behind the comforts of his royal life to seek enlightenment. At first, he went far in the opposite direction—to a life of extreme asceticism. Finally, he developed the idea of the "middle way." According to legend, he became enlightened while sitting under a giant tree. For the rest of his life he taught others, and when he died his teachings became the core of Buddhism.

Tibetan Buddhists are masters of visualization. In his book *The Bodhisattva Vow*, Geshe Kelsang Gyatso describes a visualization that includes thirty-five Buddhas, with Buddha Shakyamuni in the center on a jeweled throne supported by eight white elephants. He sits on cushions of a lotus for renunciation, a Moon for the quality of *bodhichitta* (spiritual behavior), and a Sun for wisdom. Every detail of this Buddha—his clothes, his gestures, his smile, his voice—contributes to an image so full and complex, it becomes completely realized in the person's mind. The left hand rests on his lap in a gesture of meditation. It holds a begging bowl filled with nectar, a sign of his triumph over death, delusions, and impurity. The middle finger of his right hand touches the ground, so that the Earth may witness his victory over the demons. He smiles with the love of a father for a child, and his golden body shines with light. These are only a few of the details of this intense visualization.

Buddha

Along with speech and visualization, Buddhist ritual involves prostrations. Prostrations not only show our willingness to join with the divine (see chapter 6), but also return us literally to the Earth, giving us a sense of unity with all living creatures. Gyatso describes three ways to do prostrations. You can place your whole body on the ground. You can kneel and touch the ground with your palms and forehead. Or you can form a gesture of respect, such as placing the palms together at the heart. Here, too, you may want to experience these postures and adapt them to your own rituals.

The Vietnamese Zen master Thich Nhat Hanh demonstrates the relationship between Buddhist philosophy and engagement with the world. Thich Nhat Hanh founded the Order of Interbeing in the 1960s, at the height of the Vietnam War.

Visualization

If you find yourself drawn to a particular figure—and it may be a Pagan goddess or a Christian saint as much as a Buddha—see if you can develop a precise image of this being. Begin by writing out a description or drawing it in great detail. Use color or vivid words.

When you go to sleep, place the paper nearby so you can reach it easily. In the morning, before you begin your day, look at the drawing or description, then close your eyes and imagine it as clearly as possible (if you share a bed with someone you should tell him or her ahead of time that you will be doing this and need not to be disturbed). Hold the image in your mind for ten slow deep breaths. Your mind will wander, but do not scold yourself for this. Just return each time to the image. Take one more deep breath, and as you let it out release the image and open your eyes to begin your day.

In the evening, do a more formal visualization. Find a quiet place in your house where you can sit quietly and no one will disturb you for several minutes. Set out the drawing or description on a table. Begin the practice with a small formal gesture. You might light a candle used just for this purpose. Another simple aid is a small bell that you ring once in the Buddhist manner. When you have lit the candle or rung the bell, close your eyes and breathe deeply ten times. Imagine each breath as helping to settle you and clear your mind of all the day's concerns.

After ten breaths, look at the paper. As in the morning, study it, then close your eyes and picture the image in your mind. After the ten breaths, open your eyes once more and look at the paper again. See what details you may have missed. Close your eyes and visualize it once more, for up to five minutes. Once again, as your mind wanders gently, lead it back.

Most likely you chose this figure because of some special quality. You can invoke that quality at the end of the visualization. For example, suppose you chose Kwan Yin, the Chinese goddess of compassion who has become a Buddhist deity. As you visualize her in your mind, you might say, "Kwan Yin, bring me help and guidance. Inspire me with compassion and love for those around me who are suffering." On your next deep breath, release the image. Gently blow out the candle or ring the bell to end the ritual.

If you do this every day for a week, you will discover that the figure you have chosen has become part of your own inner world. He or she will not intrude on your daily life, but you will feel a closeness, as to a friend. When you want to invoke that image and its special qualities, you will be able to do so easily.

From its beginning, the order sought to mix traditional Buddhist principles with modern social concerns.

Ritual is used to make the moral principles real and to fully inspire the members to action. Members recite the fourteen Trainings every two weeks in the form of a ceremony that includes repeated phrases, incense, bowing, and the sound of a bell.

The bell can be a very effective tool in ritual. Heard once after a statement or action, the clear sound deepens the impact. As we look at different aspects of ritual in this book, we will see how valuable this simple tool—a small bell—can be in many situations.

Judaism

As one of the world's oldest religions, Judaism is filled with ritual. To an observant traditional Jew, virtually every moment, every human action, has a sacred component and requires a blessing. To an outsider, it may seem burdensome to stop and say a short prayer before, say, eating an orange, or washing your face when you wake up. Devout Jews see these things as an opportunity. To have a blessing to say before and after food makes every meal a sacred ritual (see also chapter 7). It reminds us of the miracle of life. Novelist Cynthia Ozick has written that the observant Jew blesses the world a hundred times a day.

Judaism stresses the importance of group prayer. A service requires a *minyan* of

Torah

ten people. Each person's prayer gives strength to the others. Though many holidays mark the year, Jews actually give precedence to the Sabbath, the only sacred day listed in the Ten Commandments. Because the seventh day is a ritual, the entire week takes on a rhythm of a sacred rite.

The Sabbath ritual gains extra meaning when a boy or girl of thirteen stands before the Torah (a parchment scroll inscribed with the first five books of the Bible) for the first time in a bar mitzvah or bas mitzvah ("bar" means "son," "bas" means "daughter"; "mitzvah" is a combination of "commandment," "blessing," and "good deed"). Phyllis Berman, director of the Elat Chayyim Spiritual Center, points out that these ceremonies originally marked the onset of puberty. Over time they evolved to social and spiritual rituals for the entire family. A grandfather might present the child with a *tallis* (prayer shawl) that he himself wore at his own bar mitzvah, and which he set aside thirteen years earlier, on the child's birth. Through the chanting, the carrying of the Torah, and the interpretation

A Day of Blessings

You might want to try an experiment for a day. Be observant—that is, aware—of what you do, and for each action say a blessing. You do not need to address a specific deity. For instance, when you wake up you could simply say, "Blessed is this day in all its wonder. Blessed is my life that allows me to awaken." When you shower or wash, say a short prayer of gratitude for your health and the act of cleansing. When you eat, you could bless the plants and animals that give us food (you might find it harder to eat chemically processed food!).

When you go to work, say a blessing for the livelihood that greets you. Even if you dislike your job, try expressing gratitude for having work and an income. If you see a friend or family member, say a short blessing in your mind for having this person in your life.

To treat life this way for an entire day can change your whole outlook.

of the text, the child marks his or her entry into the adult community. For non-Jews this kind of celebration demonstrates the possibility of family and communal rituals.

American Indian

The tribal traditions of Native Americans have attracted more and more attention. For the Indians themselves, the old ways offer a return to spirituality and an answer to the poverty and hopelessness that can lead to alcoholism and other problems. This spiritual revival, very focused on rituals, has had a deep effect in many Indian nations.

For non-Indians, especially Americans, Native traditions offer a spiritual path that is close to the Earth. When we think of all that we have learned of environmental problems and the need for a different approach, we often wonder what it will take to change our behavior. Ritual can help move us beyond the intellectual awareness of issues to a real commitment to live more in harmony with our world.

Common to most Native American beliefs is the idea that Spirits act directly in the world. We feel their presence in the darkness of the sweat lodge. When we go on a Vision Quest we invite the Spirits to give us a sense of our life's mission. Indians describe their major rituals as gifts from the Spirit world rather than human inventions.

Ed McGaa, author of *Mother Earth Spirituality: Native American Paths to Healing Ourselves and Our World,* describes several rites that Native peoples across North America practice. Here are three that have become important for non-Indians as well:

1. *Otaha,* or Giveaway. The practice of giving away a dead person's belongings derived from an older ritual called The Keeping of the Soul. That rite, done a year after the death, allowed the person's spirit to remain with the family. The modern Giveaway is far more than a token ceremony. Frequently a surviving husband or wife will give out their partner's most

valuable possessions. In this way, they share wealth with the community as well as value the soul over material possessions. Giveaways also can be done with groups of living people who want to share aspects of their lives.

2. *Inipi*—the Sweat Lodge. McGaa says that a Sweat Lodge is easy to build—you can do it in a single day, with almost no money—but impossible to describe its power. In the heat of the lodge each person discovers his or her bond with Mother Earth. The very stones used gain special meaning, created millions of years ago "by the One" just for that purpose. The ritual involves music, silence, and prayer, both for each person and for the Earth. Many books on Native American religion will give instructions for building a Sweat Lodge.

3. The Vision Quest. This is the most personal of rituals, especially valuable for young people since it gives them a chance to sense their spiritual path in life. It also is very simple. Even to do it in a traditional Lakota manner you need only yourself, some twigs and four colored pieces of cloth to set out a sacred space and mark the directions, and some isolated place where you can connect yourself to nature. In the Vision Quest you devote yourself fully to that connection, without food and, unless you intend the quest to go for several days, without water. The vision itself may come in the form of a powerful dreamlike experience. The most famous example is that of Black Elk, described in John Neihardt's legendary book *Black Elk Speaks.* More likely, you will experience something more modest and subtle, but maybe just as strong—an awareness of the mystery and beauty in everything around us.

Because of the Vision Quest's simplicity and applicability to each person, many people from other traditions have adapted it to their own practices. If you wish to do a Vision Quest do not attempt anything extreme, such as a hike into deep wilderness without any prior experience. Instead, choose a place you know you can enter and leave easily, yet one that will allow you to feel a closeness to the Earth. Do not bring books or a radio or other diversion. Do bring any special objects with personal meaning for you. As you travel, especially the final walk or climb to the place, be aware of any special moments—you might see a hawk overhead, or find a beautiful rock. At the place of the quest itself, you can say prayers or do particular rituals, but there really are no special requirements other than to spend time there, stay aware of your surroundings, and ask the Earth and whatever deities you follow for a vision. As you leave, say a prayer of gratitude for whatever you have experienced, and for the Earth and your own life.

As well as ceremony, Native American religion includes personal ritual objects. These include the medicine bundle, a small bag with objects of personal power, such as a stone found on a Vision Quest and such items as sacred herbs. Another ritual object is the sacred shield, made round and divided into four quarters, with a color for each. McGaa writes that "a shield reflected the symbology of a warrior's medicine," and that such medicine included "every factor of a person's life." Thus, the shield uses symbols for love and prosperity as well as visions and dreams.

If you make a sacred shield for yourself, you can study the Lakota examples and still do it in your own way. The inner truth of the ritual is what matters most. Include on your shield (or other symbolic object) the things that symbolize your own path. If, like me, you work with Tarot cards as a spiritual teaching, your shield might include one or more cards, or your own versions of the ancient pictures.

Witchcraft

Few religions are as steeped in ritual as Witchcraft, also called Wicca. Rituals, done with joy and solemnity, magic and humor, are the prime focus of Wiccan spirituality. Almost always, these rituals blend together the ceremonial with people's actual emotions and experiences. They teach us creativity, for Wiccan rituals often link people, nature, and the goddess and god in very imaginative ways.

The modern revival of Witchcraft as a Pagan religion began in the early part of the twentieth century. In recent decades it has become a major movement, and has even been given religious tax-exempt status by the U.S. government. Wicca

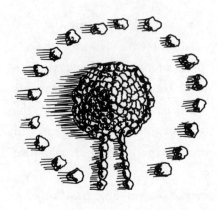

Circle of stones

honors the spirituality of women and men equally. It also celebrates the body and all of nature as sacred.

Starhawk, author of the classic *The Spiral Dance*, writes that "life is a thing of wonder" and the world is a place of joy rather than suffering. In a famous goddess poem called "The Charge of the Goddess," Doreen Valiente has the goddess declare, "All acts of love and pleasure are my rituals."

Witchcraft is wholly bound up with rituals. There are no churches or official doctrines or hierarchies. Instead, Witches operate in covens of various sizes, to a maximum of thirteen. Thirteen is a sacred number for Witches, for many rituals invoke the power of the Moon goddess, and a year contains thirteen lunations (actually 12.5, since a lunar cycle lasts 29.5 days). Each coven acts independently, with various common threads.

Starhawk describes the coven as "closer than family" (*The Spiral Dance*, p. 49), a support group, a school of mysteries, and a place of joy and magic. You don't have to follow Wicca or join a coven to become part of a ritual group. Wicca, however, gives us an example of how strong a group can become.

Wiccan ritual is magical. Starhawk writes that rituals "stimulate an awareness of the hidden side of reality, and awaken long-forgotten powers of the human mind." The power of magic does not lie in special words or actions. Instead, it comes through awareness. Through the ritual, the Craft members touch the hidden powers of transformation always present in themselves and the world around us.

Wiccans do cast spells, and sometimes for very practical things, such as finding a job. Witches will never cast spells to harm or control other people, for they have learned that whatever you send out will come back to you. This is not a moral rule so much as a psychological—and magical—truth. Thus, Witches will cast a spell to protect themselves, or to banish harm directed at them rather than attack someone who is threatening them.

Starhawk calls spell casting "lesser" magic. The "greater" is the awakening to the divine reality that plays through all existence.

Witches channel power partly through magical tools, such as a wand, a chalice, or a traditional three-legged cauldron. Chief among these is the athame, a special knife that is personal to each Witch. The athame is never used to harm or even to cut anything (except perhaps food for the feast!). It becomes an extension of the Witch's body and a kind of antenna for magical energy. Many people not strictly Wiccan have adopted the use of an athame to cut through the invisible veil separating the ordinary world and the divine.

After the magical work of the ritual comes the feasting. This can involve any food, from cookies to caviar. Wicca is a religion of reality, and food and drink are basic to life, so that the feasting is actually part of the ritual. The mood is not solemn. Starhawk stresses the importance of socializing as a way to deepen the coven. Here, too, Wicca serves as a model for any group of people who wish to do rituals together over time.

From Wicca we learn that a ritual must not just dwindle away. The members must formally close the circle. After the food and socializing, the person who began the ritual goes to the altar where she (or he) thanks the powers that have come to help them. Then she goes to the four directions and draws a "banishing pentacle" in the air to release the powers. Finally she raises her athame to the sky, touches it to the earth, then opens her arms wide to declare:

> "The circle is open, but unbroken,
> May the peace of the Goddess
> Go in our hearts
> Merry meet and merry part
> And merry meet again. Blessed be."
> (THE SPIRAL DANCE, P. 71)

We have seen how the idea of the sacred fills all rituals no matter what the tradition. And we have looked at examples from around the world and how we might apply them to our own ritual practice. We also spoke of ritual as a way to embody the sacred and make it more real. As we move deeper into the details of ritual, we will look at the senses and the way they contribute to ritual's power.

BOOKS

Berman, Phyllis Ocean and Arthur Ocean Waskow. *Tales of Tikkun.* Northvale, N.J.: Jason Aronson, 1996.

Boucher, Sandy. *Discovering Kwan Yin, Buddhist Goddess of Compassion.* Boston: Beacon Press, 1999.

Campbell, Joseph. *The Way of the Animal Powers.* New York: Times Books, 1983.

Das, Lama Surya. *Awakening to the Sacred.* New York: Broadway Books, 1999.

Gawain, Shakti. *Creative Visualization, Reissue Edition.* New York: Bantam, 1983.

Gyatso, Gershe Gelsang. *The Bodhisattva Vow, Second Edition.* Pocklington, U.K.: Tharpa, 1996.

Hanh, Thich Nhat. *Interbeing, Third Edition.* Berkeley, Calif.: Parallax, 1998.

Jung, Carl Gustav. R. F. Hull, Translator. G. Adler, Editor. *Synchronicity: An Acausal Connecting Principle.* Princeton, N.J.: Princeton University Press, 1988.

Khan, Pir Vilayat. *Eyes of God: A Sufi Initiation.* New York: Tarcher, 1999.

Linn, Denise. *Quest: A Guide to Creating Your Own Vision Quest.* New York: Ballantine Wellspring, 1999.

McGaa, Ed, Eagle Man. *Mother Earth Spirituality.* San Francisco: HarperSanFrancisco, 1990.

Neihardt, John G. Introduction by Vine Deloria, Jr. *Black Elk Speaks.* Lincoln, Neb.: University of Nebraska Press, 1988.

Rumi, Jalal Al-Dinn. Deepak Chopra, Editor. Fereydoun Kia, Translator. *The Love Poems of Rumi.* New York: Harmony Books, 1998.

Somé, Malidoma Patrice. *Of Water and the Spirit.* New York: Penguin, 1994.

Starhawk. *The Spiral Dance, 10th Anniversary Edition.* San Francisco: HarperSanFrancisco, 1989.

Stone, Merlin. *When God Was a Woman.* New York: Harcourt Brace, 1978.

Teish, Luisa. *Jambalaya: The Natural Woman's Book of Personal Charms and Practical Rituals, Reprint Edition.* San Francisco: HarperSanFrancisco, 1988.

Toibin, Colm. *The Sign of the Cross.* New York: Vintage, 1996.

Tzo, Lao. Translated by Ursula Leguin. *Tao Te Ching.* Boston: Shambhala, 1998.

Wimala, Bhante. *Lessons of the Lotus.* New York: Bantam, 1997.

THESE ILLUSTRATED BOOKS SHOW THE PAGEANTRY OF
THE WORLD'S TRADITIONAL RITUALS

Ginn, Victoria. *The Spirited Earth: Dance, Myth, and Ritual from South Asia to the South Pacific.*
New York: Rizzoli, 1990.

Powell, Andrew. Photographs by Graham Harrison. Foreword by His Holiness the
Dalai Lama. *Living Buddhism.* Berkeley, Calif.: University of California Press,
1989.

Smith, Huston. *Illustrated World's Religions.* New York: HarperCollins, 1995 (pb).

THE FOLLOWING AUDIO PROGRAMS FOCUS ON A
PARTICULAR TRADITION AND ITS RITUALS

Buddhism
Kornfield, Jack. *Your Buddha Nature.*

Rinpoche, Sogyal. *Tibetan Wisdom for Living and Dying.*

Christianity
Harvey, Andrew. *Radiant Heart: The Radical Teachings of Jesus and the Christian Mystics.*

Eco-spirituality
Swimme, Brian. *Canticle to the Cosmos.*

Milton, John P. *Sky Above, Earth Below.*

Hinduism
Dass, Ram. *Experiments in Truth.*

Islam
Vaughan-Lee, Llewellyn. *Love Is a Fire and I Am Wood: The Sufi's Mystical Journey Home.*

Judaism
Cooper, Rabbi David. *The Mystical Kabbalah.*

All audio programs, among many others, available from Sounds True
(800–333–9185).

Two

❖

Ritual and the Senses

3.

Sight

Having taken a whirlwind tour of rituals around the world, we will take another journey, this time through the senses. Ritual is powerful because it involves us on so many different levels—the intellectual, the imaginative, but especially the sensual. To gain a greater understanding of this, we will look at the different senses and how we experience them in ritual practices. Once again, we will consult the teachers who have dedicated their lives to spiritual awakening. And once again, we will find ways to use traditional examples in our own lives.

We begin with the very sense you are using right now to read this book—sight.

Hundreds of candles to the Virgin Mary flicker in the back of the massive cathedral. The setting sun lights up the stained-glass windows on the west wall with vivid scenes of the Savior.

Brilliant silk flags flap in the breeze. Beyond them stand the jagged peaks of the world's highest mountains. Lines of monks in saffron robes march under the bright spin of the prayer wheels.

In the austere desert, the shaman's brightly colored costume stands out like an exotic flower. The huge eyes of the mask seem to roll like spinning comets, while the red tongue hangs out, thirsty for the spiritual wine of the gods.

The long, narrow hall is lined on either side with tier upon tier of golden Buddhas, some a few inches high, some larger than life, some dancing, some contemplative. At the end rises Kwan Yin, Chinese Bodhisattva of mercy, her one hundred arms fanning out on either side like the wings of an angel.

These are just a few of the marvelous ways people have fed their hunger for visions of divine experience. Of all the senses, sight is the one that makes the greatest impression. "Seeing is believing," we say, for when we behold something it becomes real.

Loving the Image

Tarot use relies heavily on sight, for it is not the symbolism or the predictive formulas that make Tarot cards special, but the images themselves. If we really want to know the cards and their value, we need to return again and again to the pictures. In my classes we describe them, we tell stories about them, we paint them, we act them out, we invite them into our imaginations, we even perform a ritual (see Introduction) in which everyone becomes a Tarot card. I call this "loving the image," and it applies to a great deal more than Tarot cards. You can approach all ritual this way, reverent and playful at the same time.

To love the image means simply to stay with the actual picture or description of a being or sacred symbol rather than all the philosophical or symbolic meanings we attach to them. Meanings are important, but the simple act of looking can be powerful in its own right.

Moments in Stone

When we go to sacred sites, such as Stonehenge, it is first of all the sight that draws us, the huge stone pillars in a circle on the top of a hill. I have visited Stonehenge several times, once without an actual plan. A friend and I were on our way to another sacred site in England, the prehistoric hill known as Glastonbury Tor. It was a rainy afternoon, and as we came around a bend, there stood Stonehenge in the distance, alone and somber under the gray sky. Feeling as if a magnet pulled us, we turned the car onto the side road and headed for the stones.

Stonehenge, and many other prehistoric monuments, were actually created for visual effect. On the longest day of the year, the Summer Solstice, the first rays of the sun coming over the horizon behind Stonehenge pass between two stones to strike a flat stone in the center, called the "heelstone." So impressive is this sight that every year the British government has to guard Stonehenge to prevent thousands of people crowding it to glimpse that magic moment. The authorities do, however, allow the Druids, descendants of Celtic pre-Christian priests, to go there and perform an ancient ritual—the marking of the turning of the light on the longest day of the year.

An even more impressive visual effect takes place in Ireland, exactly six months later, on the Winter Solstice, at a giant human-made mound called Newgrange. Thousands of years old, Newgrange is as large as a small hill. A stone entryway opens to a long narrow passage, with two side chambers that give the interior the form of a cross. The passageway itself is a stunning sight, the stones so perfectly fit together they have kept their form, without cement of any kind, for millennia. At the back wall, the corbeled roof of the artificial cave rises high above your head, one huge stone overlapping another to form a beehive of rock. But still more remarkable is what happens on the midwinter sunrise. Shortly after dawn, a beam of light enters the passageway. Over several minutes it moves slowly across the floor until finally it reaches the back wall, which it climbs to a height higher than a man, remains for several minutes, then retreats out of the mouth of the cave.

The Points of the Year

These and many other phenomenal feats of Stone Age engineering and surveying allowed people to mark the turning points of the year. Some people maintain this was done simply to mark the proper times for planting and harvesting. But midsummer and midwinter are not significant dates for agriculture. They are important in that they mark turning points in the year. We can imagine Stonehenge and Newgrange as great ritual centers where people would come on pilgrimage from many miles around to honor the gods of the seasons. Before electric lights and weather forecasts, such rituals helped people follow nature's rhythms.

Today, people still honor these special days of extreme light and darkness in visual ways. At the Summer Solstice, people will wear white to match the brilliance of the Sun. In the Winter, they will carry torches. In a small town near my home, people parade to a river in Winter, carrying brightly colored banners. At the water's edge, they float candles on miniature ice boats to bring light into the darkness. In this way they invite the light of hope and belief into whatever dark areas they may experience in their own lives.

Rock Art

Thousands of years before Stonehenge, our earliest ancestors also used images for ritual. As long as thirty, forty, even fifty thousand years ago, in places as far away as southern France and the Australian desert, people painted intense scenes and figures on cave and rock walls. One of the most powerful of these is the cave of Lascaux in France. Though it has been closed to the general public since 1964 (to avoid decay of the pictures), I have had the great good fortune to visit there. A guide took me underground to an antechamber, where he turned off all light but a single bulb at ground level, which gave off no more illumination than a night-light. Then he led me into the main hall and turned on the full light. Though I had seen photographs of Lascaux many times and knew a little of what to expect, I will never forget that moment.

Imagine that in the heat of summer initiates were taken down into the dark, cold rock with only a small torch for illumination. At the right moment the priests/shamans would have fired up the larger torches. Suddenly, the initiates would have seen one of the world's most astonishing sights—a long, narrow stone chamber filled with huge paintings of bulls and horses. In bright lines of black and yellow and red, they run and leap and even fall across the rock walls, some as long as nineteen feet from tail to horns, one on top of another, all of them in vibrant detail, their bodies and faces all but alive. In the presence of such magnificence the initiates must have believed themselves magically transported to the world of what Joseph Campbell called "the Animal Powers."

Geometry and Symbols

Basic forms of symbolism often come from nature. The most common natural form, found in such creatures as snails, the movement of water, and the shape of galaxies, is the spiral. Because they turn around and around but eventually open up, spirals suggest evolution and becoming. The circle appears visibly in nature only in the Sun and the Full Moon. This gives the circle a special otherworldly quality, a symbol of divine perfection, unchanging and radiant.

Straight lines do not appear in nature at all, except in one circumstance—when a cloud partly hides the Sun but allows rays of light to emerge. This gives straight lines the quality of abstract thought and single-mindedness.

The five-pointed star, or pentagram, may seem like an abstract image. But if you stand with your legs apart and your arms out, you will discover that the pentagram actually symbolizes the human body. There are other pentagrams in nature. Many flowers have five petals. Over eight years, the planet Venus follows a pattern in our sky like a five-petaled flower. If you cut an apple in half across the middle, you will discover a perfect five-pointed star. Thus, the pentagram is special because it unites the human body, the plant world, and the brightest object in the sky after the Sun and Moon.

Color and Ritual

Color can enhance ritual in many ways. It brings qualities of beauty and sensual excitement that deepen the impact of ritual's words and actions. By making an effort to include color, we involve ourselves more in the preparation. When we make an extra effort, we get more from the ritual itself.

Color is also important because of its effect upon us. Color is actually a particular vibration of light. Many people believe that each color frequency affects us in particular ways. Some healers will use colored lights to activate particular energy in the body and then will tell their clients to surround themselves with that color for a period of time. For example, if the person needs red he or she might wear red clothes and scarves, put fresh roses in the house, even eat red foods, such as strawberries. Doing ritual with a particular color can be a powerful way to boost the effect.

Color, Chakras, and the Rainbow

One special way to understand the importance of color comes from yoga. Yoga teaches that the body contains seven centers—or knots—of energy called "chakras." The basic life energy known as kundalini lies coiled at the base of the spine. Enlightenment comes when the kundalini rises through the different chakras to the top of the head, called the "crown." Each chakra is aligned with a color. Clairvoyants who can see auras look at the strength or weakness of the colors around a person's chakras to see where he or she is strong or weak. The colors are the same as the rainbow: red, the color of blood and thus survival, at the bottom, or root, chakra; orange at the sacral, or genital, area; yellow at the solar plexus (when we breathe in properly we breathe in the Sun's yellow life energy down to the solar plexus); green, the color of plants, at the heart; blue at the throat; indigo at the third eye (center of the forehead); and violet at the crown. However, in the rainbow red is at the top and violet at the bottom, so that if we want to align our bodies with the rainbows we have to stand on our heads! This is one reason why yoga includes headstands, and why a central card of the Tarot deck, the Hanged Man, shows the figure hanging upside down by one foot.

Each chakra, and therefore each color, has a special quality. Red is survival, orange is desire, yellow is centeredness, green is emotion, blue is communication, indigo is psychic awareness, and violet is spiritual attainment. If you do yoga, or Indian meditation, you can use specific chakra colors in ritual to activate specific energies.

Color Symbolism

As well as direct physical properties, specific colors have symbolic meanings. To some extent, this depends on culture. For example, to most people in the United States, white means purity and perfection and happiness. Black means negativity, depression, even death. Brides wear white for the ritual of the wedding to symbolize purity and virginity. At funerals people wear black as a symbol of their grief. In old movies the good guys wore white hats and the bad guys black. These qualities are so ingrained in our cultural beliefs that we think of them as natural. And yet in many Asian cultures white symbolizes death. The absence of specific colors suggests emptiness, and so they dress the corpse in white. In China, brides wear red, because it symbolizes health and prosperity. And in some Native American cultures, black means life, because black dirt is the most fertile.

Does all this mean we should throw up our hands and not use color at all because there are no absolute meanings? In ritual, intent matters a great deal. This means that we can decide ahead of time what colors symbolize for us, and how they will affect us when we use them. And if you are following a specific tradition that uses color symbolically, by all means accept that system as real.

You also can develop your own color symbolism. Does yellow, the color of the Sun, make you feel alert and happy? Then make sure to include yellow in rituals to express the joy of life. You could color a ritual table in yellow cloth, or set out yellow flowers. Do you instinctively think of white as light and black as darkness?

Then use them that way in your rituals. Perhaps you might want to experiment with black as a way to overcome any fears of the dark.

Certain colors do suggest meanings by the way they appear in life. Red is the color of blood. In horror movies red may be used to scare people, but on the level of ritual red evokes life energy, vitality, action. Light blue is the color of the sky on a bright day and so can evoke calm and simplicity, qualities we feel on pleasant days. Dark blue, on the other hand, is the color of the sea and of deep twilight. Therefore, for many people dark blue represents the hidden depths of the self. Dark blue in a ritual would aid meditation, or an introspective look at our lives. We can pair red and blue as opposites. Red is assertive and outgoing, whereas blue is quiet and receptive. Red is forceful, blue is intuitive. Because purple combines these two basic colors, it can symbolize balance and attainment of a state where we combine strong personality with inner peace.

The Power of Altars

An altar is a physical space we set aside to decorate for ritual use. An altar is a place of inspiration and encounters with the divine. We create them, and use them, in simple or complex rituals to allow this to happen. This goes for altars we make in our homes as much as it does for the altars in a cathedral. Robert Farris Thompson, author of *Face of the Gods: Art and Altars of Africa and the African-Americans*, writes, "The altar is a school of being, designed to attract and deepen the power of inspiration." And he quotes Gazon Matoja, a traditional ruler of the Ndjuta Maroons of Suriname, South America (Maroons were escaped slaves who set up their own culture, mixing African and Indian traditions): "An altar is a place where you realize your beliefs." Peg Streep, author of *Altars Made Easy*, a handbook of altar techniques and symbolism, describes an altar as "a physical place where the divine can be glimpsed or experienced." Streep points out that altars don't make sacred space. They release what is already there.

This is true in places of mysterious power, such as established sacred sites, where you might do your own ritual and connect to the power already honored.

It's true among the trees and rocks of your backyard, where you may wish to release the sacredness of your own feeling for nature. And it's true in your bedroom or living room, and even, as Streep points out, in your office, where a small altar on your desk can heal the artificial split between spirituality and daily life, as well as energize your job and help increase harmony with workmates.

We will look at altars in some detail, for they can form a vital part of our own ritual practice, both alone and in groups.

Altars Out of Everyday Objects

Studying the sacred imagery of other cultures can help us see some of our own possibilities. We all have seen motorcycles and customized cars with flames painted on them, pictures of animals, devils, and so on. What does someone feel when he rides off on a motorcycle painted with eagles and fiery cougars? Thompson describes the way African-American artists will transform a car into a conscious altar of African symbolism, often based on the idea of the soul's journey through life back to the Spirit world. Thus, an artist named Charles Chisolm decorated a motorcycle with 1,450 lightbulbs and 3,500 rhinestones.

You do not need expensive or rare objects to create an altar. Africans will use such things as dinner plates, or even iron nails. Consider how you might make an altar from everyday things. You could find antique plates in a secondhand shop, maybe with flowers to symbolize abundance, and then paint them with symbols you find meaningful. A doll could symbolize childhood memories, especially if you put photographs alongside it. Or you could dress a doll in clothes symbolic of something you desire in your life—a wedding dress for a woman who wants to meet a life partner, something symbolic of a profession for work. Altars do not have to be overly serious to be meaningful. Layers of brightly colored cloth will add beauty and a sense of depth.

Ritual Altars in Your Own Front Yard

Altars do not have to be indoors. You might want to decorate some aspect of your property—for example, a tree—as an altar. Here are some steps to create a tree altar:

1. Choose the tree carefully. An oak embodies great strength. An evergreen shows the power of life throughout the year. You might choose a silver birch for the beauty of its bark. You can write or paint on birch bark, so that with birch you can double the ritual by painting a symbolic image on the bark and either leaving it on the tree or bringing it into an altar inside the house. This last action creates a current of energy between the outer and inner shrines. Be careful to use bark that's already separated itself from the tree, lest you cause harm.

2. Sometimes you can find a tree whose trunk has separated at the base into two or more trees growing from the same roots. A double trunk might symbolize partnership or marriage. A triple trunk can become a shrine to the triple goddess of Pagan tradition. Such multiple trunks symbolize the many emerging from the one, and are good for group rituals. My own property contains a tree root that has split into five separate trunks. I have used it as a shrine to the many goddesses connected to the planet Venus, with its fivefold pattern—Aphrodite, Venus, Inanna, Astarte, and others.

3. Gather the materials you want to use. These could include streamers in a symbolic color (see pp. 55–56), crystals, small dolls, miniature statues of goddesses or gods, symbols such as stars or crosses, Runes or Tarot cards, and personal items, such as a toy from childhood, or photographs of family members.

4. The more consciously you do this, the more powerful the altar will become. In other words, don't just grab some things and stick them on the tree when you have a spare moment between errands. Creating a visual shrine is not simply another item on the to-do lists all of us carry. Assemble your offerings carefully, and think about them.

5. Set aside a special time. You might want to wait for one of the solar days, such as an Equinox.

6. Carry the objects to the tree with a sense of solemnity. You can do this alone or with friends, possibly chanting or playing instruments. As you hang each piece, or set it at the base of the tree, do so consciously. You can state its purpose: "Let this crystal bring the light of Spirit into my home. Let this mirror reflect all hardship away from me and my family. Let this picture of my grandmother inspire us with love."

7. When you have finished, eat something, perhaps a small cake, scatter a few crumbs at the base of the tree, and drink some wine or juice after pouring some on the roots.

8. After you have done the ritual, each time you look at the tree—through the window, or on your way to work—you will sense the power it continues to generate.

9. Because a tree shrine is outdoors and part of a living creature, it will change. Some things will blow away or fall apart. This becomes part of its beauty. As it transforms, it becomes an emblem of your inner growth.

Home Altars

Your altar is you. It helps define and clarify who you are spiritually and emotionally. By creating something outside yourself, in the form of an aesthetic arrangement of objects, you learn about yourself. You also make a commitment to your growth. The altar becomes a place to perform private rituals—from lighting candles to saying prayers to bowing to the deities to offering food (Chinese altars, whether in temples or homes, always include fresh fruit). And each time you do a ritual, or meditate before it, you give it greater power, power that then becomes available to you in your daily life. This is not a case of surrendering power but of increasing it. Your altar can become an important source of personal strength to get you through difficult times, a place you return to for solace or inner renewal.

Some people change their altars every day. If you read Tarot cards or Runes, you might choose one each morning and set it on your altar so you both take it into your sacred space and let it radiate out from that spiritual center into your day. If you do affirmations (see chapter 4), you might write the affirmation on a card and set it on your altar. You can place photos of people in your life on your altar. You can add small gifts that have special meaning, or objects you discover, or a drawing or letter or journal entry.

A time of sickness will bring forth candles plus written prayers, or statues of such figures as Kwan Yin, the Chinese goddess of mercy, or the Virgin Mary. Some people never remove anything from their altar. They prefer the layers of meaning to become denser and denser, the altar a record of their lives. Others like simplicity, and will take away objects and symbols that no longer feel as potent to them.

When you create an altar somewhere in your house, your entire home becomes more meaningful.

Placing Your Altar

Many people situate their home altars by convenience, such as on the top of a dresser, or on a small table in a corner. You also might arrange your altar according to the four directions. As we have seen, there is no single tradition of meaning for the directions, but Peg Streep suggests the following basic symbolism, which will work in most places in the Northern Hemisphere. North symbolizes cool rational thought; South brings in passion; East gives us new possibilities, hope, inspiration, and youth; West opens to quiet and resolution, solitude and old age. If you wish to bring out particular qualities in yourself, you could create an altar, with suitable symbols and images, on the side of the room for the correct direction. Or you could seek balance, and set up your altar with areas for each direction. Because you change it from time to time, you could periodically emphasize one area over another.

The Medicine Wheel

One cultural tradition that uses the directions of the compass in a special way is the Native American Medicine Wheel. Like the Buddhist mandala, the Medicine Wheel is a depiction of the cosmos, with ourselves in the center, supported by Mother Earth below and Father Sky above. It consists of a circle quartered into four sections, each one aligned to one of the four cardinal directions.

You can paint a medicine wheel on cloth and lay it out as an altar on the floor for rituals that invoke the directions. After you draw the circle and quarter it, paint in the colors. For further symbols, you can paint on images or lay actual objects on the quadrants.

Each direction contains a particular stone and an animal. The stones generate particular kinds of energy, while the animals embody special qualities that we want to bring out in ourselves. Think of those bulls and horses painted on the walls of Lascaux cave. In Western cultures, children automatically feel the power of animals. Because we do not encourage this natural tendency, children "grow out" of this relationship and we lose the complex spiritual understanding our ancestors had of the other creatures of the Earth.

In her book *Buffalo Woman Comes Singing,* Native American shaman and teacher Brooke Medicine Eagle gives one version of the stones and animals for each direction:

East—the color yellow. Its stone is amber, its animal the golden eagle.

West—deep brown and black. The stone is obsidian, the animal the black bear or the raven.

South—red, with the stone the carnelian or garnet, and the animal the coyote.

North—the place of clarity. Its color is white, its stone the clear crystal (including diamonds), and its animal the white owl.

The Medicine Wheel image also helps us to organize where we place our altar and what we put on it. If you decide to place your altar on the north wall of a room, you might want such things as white objects or cloth, a picture of an owl, a crystal, or a bowl of clear water.

Healing Altars

Many people create altars for healing. The simplest of these is a long-burning candle and a photograph of the person. Such candles, in tall glass jars, are a Mexican tradition, and you can find them in the Hispanic foods section of many large supermarkets. Mexicans use candles for many purposes, and the candles will sometimes contain images of saints, or the Virgin Mary, or theme words such as "Prosperity" or "Love." Obviously you can use these, or untitled candles, for these specific purposes, but you also can use such candles for your own ritual ideas, in particular healing. Things you can add to rituals for healing are something special to the sick person, some memento of your connection to the person, healing prayers and affirmations written on cards, and pictures of gods or goddesses dedicated to health. (For more on healing rituals, see chapter 9.)

Drive along a winding road and you are likely to see, somewhere on a curve, a small cross or a pile of stones. There may be flowers, personal mementos, a framed photograph, and sometimes a covered oil lamp that will burn in all weather. These are memorials to people killed in car accidents. They allow the person's friends and family to remember someone they loved at the place of death. They express sadness and a silent outrage, at fate or a badly cared for road. And they warn other drivers to slow down, to not drive when drunk.

If you and a friend or relative have suffered a painful split, the two of you can do a healing ritual before an altar that you create jointly. Each of you brings something precious of your own, and something that for you represents the other person, especially a positive memory of them. You might symbolically reenact the incident, maybe switching roles. You can follow this performance with actions symbolic of the willingness to heal the anger. At the end, lighting one candle with two matches will signify the return of love.

Children and Ritual Creativity

Children love ritual. They love its drama, its quality of make-believe, and especially its creativity. The visual aspect of ritual often appeals to children the most, with its chance to create bright fantasy-filled altars or robes or special objects. Children are natural creators. They will dig out old toys, or forage in the woods for special stones or sticks, or pick wildflowers to decorate a table. Rituals that include fire, such as a bonfire on the Summer Solstice, are especially exciting for children.

The mandala

The things we do with children are not trivial or less spiritual. Often the best possibilities come from ancient traditions that happen to involve activities children enjoy. Following are two examples.

In places as diverse as Tibet and Navaho country, people make elaborate drawings with colored sand to use in communal rituals. Buddhist monks in Tibet and Nepal will spend weeks creating vast intricate mandalas whose brilliant colors and complex geometry decribe the entire cosmos. In Navaho country, sand drawings are dancing grounds for ritual initiations. The paintings take the form of stylized Spirit beings, so that the dancers dance their way through the gods' very bodies.

Sand paintings or sculptures are a wonderful medium for children, who will think of sand castles at the beach. You can use colored sand (often available in craft stores) for drawing. Just sprinkle the sand one color at a time to make lines and shapes. You can do this on the ground outdoors, or even on a tabletop.

At the beach, or even in a sandbox, you and your children can wet the sand to sculpt it. You also can add special objects, such as "magical" rocks or shells that the child can choose, or small statues or crystals. If an outside area is safe for this purpose, you could burn candles, or make a small fire at the edge of the sand creation. The transitory quality of the sand, especially at the beach, will give your actions a special poignancy.

The second method with children involves decorating trees or branches to create Spirit guardians. This idea comes from the Salteau Indians of Saskatchewan, who dress trees or stick figures with clothes and pasted-on hair or beards to create what they call *manitokanac*. The Indians do as little carving as possible, preferring to find wood with the natural suggestion of a human form or face. The manitokanac are like scarecrows. But where a scarecrow is purely functional, the manitokan invites, or calls forth, a Spirit to guard the home and make it sacred. Choosing and dressing a tree Spirit is another natural activity to do with children, who will think of Halloween dummies as well as scarecrows.

Go together to find the right branch or tree. Look for a natural form that calls to you with its energy. If it's a tree, you can dress and decorate it right where it is. If it is a branch or a log, you could take it indoors or set it before the entrance. You can use crystals or mirrors for eyes. You can dress the tree in ritual robes or simply wrap it in bright cloth. When you have finished, lead your children in a prayer to the Spirit who will enter it and bless your home. You also should say a blessing for the Salteaux Indians, whose tradition has inspired this idea.

Finally, you can create indoor altars with your children. This can be both a creative and a bonding experience. It also can help lure your child away from the TV or video games. Children will help you pick which objects from your own collection should go where on your altar. They also will bring their own dolls or old toys (decide ahead of time whether you will accept Barbie or GI Joe alongside your precious jade Buddha; before you reject the idea, ask yourself, "What might the Buddha think of my child's offering?"). Once you and your child have built your altars, they become wonderful places to do further rituals for such events as the first day of school. You can do such simple actions as giving thanks, or pouring wine or juice into a special glass set on the altar.

Sight is crucial in ritual, because it gives us vivid settings that allow us to shape our ceremonies and their symbolic meanings. But sight, of course, is only one of the senses. In the following chapter, we will look at sight's partner, sound, and the ways chants, and words, and even silence affect us as we explore the truths of ritual.

Cornell, Judith. *Mandala: Luminous Symbols for Healing.* Wheaton, Ill.: Quest Books, 1995.

Grey, Alex. Foreword by Ken Wilbur. *The Mission of Art.* Boston: Shambhala, 1998.

Hawkins, Gerald. *Stonehedge Decoded.* New York: Dell, 1965.

Leidy, Denise P. and Robert Thurman. *Mandala.* Boston: Shambhala, 1997.

Medicine Eagle, Brooke. *Buffalo Woman Comes Singing.* New York: Ballantine, 1991.

Raspoli, Mario. *Lascaux, The Final Photographs.* New York: Abrams, 1986.

Streep, Peg. *Altars Made Easy.* San Francisco: HarperSanFrancisco, 1997.

Walker, Barbara. *The Woman's Dictionary of Symbols and Sacred Objects.* San Francisco: HarperSanFrancisco, 1988.

Yun, Ling and Sarah Rossbach. *Living Color.* New York: Kodansha, 1994.

IF YOU WISH TO CREATE YOUR OWN ART FOR AN ALTAR OR RITUAL, THE FOLLOWING BOOKS ARE USEFUL GUIDES

Cameron, Julia. *The Artist's Way.* New York: Tarcher, 1992.

Ganim, Barbara. *Art and Healing.* New York: Three Rivers Press, 1999.

Gold, Aviva. *Painting from the Source.* New York: HarperPerennial, 1998.

WEB SITES

See the Artist's Way at Work home site for on-line creativity support groups, www.artistswaywork.com.

For visual images of the Tibetan Mandala constructed at the Museum of Fine Arts in Houston, see www.chron.com.

4.

Sound

The drums begin slowly. They enter your body so that you cannot help but move. As they pick up speed, all your ordinary thoughts and hesitations fly away from you like beads of sweat.

The chant is low and insistent. At first you cannot follow the words, but soon you pick them up. As you and the group repeat the short phrase over and over, you feel your spirit rise and fly.

The monks kneel before the great peaks of the Himalayas. Over and over they chant the names of the Buddhas and Bodhisattvas. A single stroke of the brass bell sends a piercing note to vibrate through the mountains. The echoes fill the sky like a choir.

Varied Uses

Whether we realize it or not, we all have grown up with ritual sounds. If you were raised in a religious tradition, you probably remember some hymn or prayer from your childhood. If you were raised in a secular way, chances are you still sang Christmas carols with friends; the grace of such songs as "Silent Night" gives them a special power even for people without a Christian background. Perhaps your mother taught you something special to say every night before going to sleep, or you might have gone to high school football games and cried the school chant for victory. Or shouted a slogan over and over in an antiwar march, or locked arms with a group of people to sing "We Shall Overcome."

Small hand drum

These are just a few of the many ways we use sound to deepen ritual experience. But no particular sense can occur in isolation. When we considered sight, we described how people will say blessings at their altar—sound—and use movement as they bow to the divine images. Here, too, the sound of prayer, or the invocation of Spirit, is reinforced by the majesty of a cathedral, or the bright colors of a temple, or banners that you and your ritual companions put up to define sacred space in your own home. Drums are not used for their sound alone. They create movement, and the movement itself becomes heightened through swirls of silk, or feathered headdresses, or giant masks.

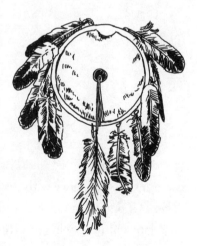

In many ways, sound is the most varied of the senses in ritual. It encompasses everything from a poetic prayer to guttural cries to loud exhalations of breath to choirs of drums to the eerie drone of a didgeridoo. All of these and many more take us from our ordinary reality to the discovery of the sacred.

Feathered shield

A Hum for Peace

Can we really measure the full power of sound? Ed McGaa, in his discussion of ceremony, reminds us of a worldwide ritual that occurred in August 1987. Astronomers had
determined that an unusual alignment of heavenly bodies would take place on August
16 and 17. People all over the world decided to gather in small groups to do their own
rituals for harmony and peace. The organizers of this movement knew that no set of
actions, no single prayer, no matter how simple, could possibly work for people of
vastly different languages and cultures. So they hit upon something so basic that
everyone would know it. At a certain time they asked people across the world simply
to hum. Hum alone or in groups, with melodies or tunes. Just hum. Could such an act
do anything? McGaa points out that within two years the Berlin Wall fell, and one of the
world's most repressive empires simply fell to pieces, virtually without a single shot.
Most people would say that these things happened through political forces. But all
change happens through its outer manifestations. And those political forces were as
unprecedented as hundreds of thousands of people all across the world humming
together.

The Power of Names

According to Hindu and Jewish traditions, the Creator used sound to bring the
world into being. The Hindu Brahma begins the world with a syllable. The Hebrew
Elohim starts existence with the famous sentence "Let there be light." After creating
Adam, God gives him the task of naming the other creatures of the Earth.

Many cultures believe in the power of names. Some people have used a public
name and kept their true name secret to prevent anyone working a spell against
them. Ancient Jews believed that God's secret name was so powerful that only the
High Priest could pronounce it, and then only once a year, on the Day of
Atonement, inside the Holy of Holies in the center of the temple. Even today,
Jews refer to God as *HaShem*, "the Name."

In Western culture today, many people's names are chosen for their sound, without thought to the name's original meaning. People named Isaac have no idea the name comes from the Hebrew for "laughter." How many women named Val realize the name means "courage" in Latin? Often, if we learn the original meaning of our name we discover a quality in it that we recognize in ourselves. Some people also take on a new name, one whose meaning expresses something they wish to bring out in their lives.

Ed McGaa writes about the power of receiving a "natural" name—that is, a descriptive name based on nature. He describes it as "comforting" to have an explicit link to Mother Earth. His book *Mother Earth Spirituality* includes a list of actual names received in ceremony by both Native Americans and "rainbow" people ("rainbow" is McGaa's name for non-Indians who wish to follow the "Red Path"). They include "Children's Warrior Woman," "Eagle of the Spirit Water," "Laughing Heart," and so on. Such names are more powerful when given in ritual. For Indians this may occur in a Sweat Lodge when an elder looks into the person's spirit and solemnly pronounces the natural name.

Affirmations

We also use the sound of words in affirmations. These are short, positive phrases we say about ourselves to change the negative lessons we've absorbed from what *other* people have said about us. To make this reprogramming work, we need to hear the affirmation out loud, ten or fifteen times, a couple of times a day, for two weeks.

Mary K. Greer, author of *Tarot for Yourself*, describes affirmations as a way of empowering people after a Tarot reading. She asks the person to choose a card that represents the qualities the person would like to develop in her- or himself. When the person has chosen a picture, Greer asks the person to describe these qualities in her or his own terms. The person may say, "This card shows someone who's strong and gentle and fulfills her dreams." They then work together to create a single positive sentence, staying as close as possible to the person's own words. The sentence should stay in the present. Not "I will," but "I am." "My gentle strength fulfills my dreams."

Your Own Naming Ceremony

You can conduct your own naming ritual, with a simple minimum of two people. Here is one based on a mutual naming ceremony I attended in Amsterdam, the Netherlands:

1. People sit in pairs facing each other. Everyone should have some paper and crayons or markers near at hand. Whether there are two people or thirty, one person should act as leader, to decide the right moment for each step.

2. Begin with a calming exercise to release your intuitive senses. This can be as simple as everyone sitting quietly and breathing deeply. A small bell rung once at the beginning of the session can help everyone settle into the ritual.

3. When the leader senses that the group is ready, she or he rings the bell softly a second time to begin the next stage. Everyone opens their eyes and looks deeply into the eyes of the person across from them. As much as they can, they seek to forget their own concerns and seek only the truth of the other person. If your mind wanders, bring it back to the person across from you. Stay focused on the eyes.

4. After approximately five minutes, the leader rings the bell once more. Now people take up the paper and crayons and draw as vivid a picture as they can of some image that represents what they saw in the other person.

5. When the picture is done, write a name on the paper. The name may have come spontaneously while looking at the person, or else it may derive from the picture.

6. Each person says the name she or he has given the other, and the other repeats it. When we say something we make it more real, no longer just an idea but a part of the world. This, too, is the power of sound.

7. At the sound of the bell, everyone closes their eyes for a final deep breath. They repeat their new names silently to themselves. The bell rings once more to end the ritual.

8. In future rituals, or even social situations, you and your naming partner will share a special bond. You have named each other.

Greer asks the person to write this down and tape it on the bathroom mirror or somewhere else where she will see it every day, so that she can repeat it out loud morning and evening. Greer also asks the person to think of one concrete action she can take toward her goal in the next twenty-four hours.

Notice the different elements in play here. The card itself is a visual trigger. It allows the reader and the "querent" to explore just what the person needs in her life. The action takes this out of the realm of wishful longing and begins to make it real. And the sound of her own voice as she repeats the affirmation each day

Ritual Vows

Things said out loud take on special value. Things said in a ritual context take on great power. Ritual statements spoken with ceremonial movement followed by other sounds to reinforce the words become still more significant. And when we do this in the presence of a master, the statements can transform our lives. In chapter 2, we saw how Thich Nhat Hanh founded his Order of Interbeing to counter the civil war and bombs in Vietnam with communities dedicated to tolerance and love. The vows and the teachings carry the power to overcome violence through complex rituals, including incense, prostrations, and the pure sound of the bell. In one ritual the head of the ceremony says, "May we waken from forgetfulness and realize our true home." The sound of the bell after this statement can indeed awaken this truth within us.

Is there some commitment you need to make to yourself? Some step you know you need to take but have put off for a long time? Consider making a vow in the midst of a sacred ritual.

Suppose you have vacillated for a long time over changing your career. You would like to dedicate yourself to music, you have had enough success to believe you can do it, but you have feared the insecurity. A New Year's or Solstice ritual might be a good time to make a vow. Perhaps the ritual climaxes in a bonfire to signal that new life energy will emerge out of the flames of the old. As the fire roars into life, you say to yourself, "I vow to live and support myself by my true work." To seal the vow with an action, you throw several grains of cornmeal into the flames.

will deepen the belief. The more we work with such things as Tarot cards and indeed ritual itself, the more we realize that we do not desire things that are completely alien to ourselves. If we seek "gentle strength," it is because we already possess it. We just need to bring it out from inside ourselves.

The Sounds of Silence

We live in a world full of noise. Television commercials, arguments, answering machines, call waiting, meetings, parties, book groups, records, movies, and on and on. It all comes from outside, a bombardment. How often do we sit in silence to listen to our inner selves? How often do we give ourselves the chance to discover the spiritual truths inside us? Dr. Andrew Weil, author of several books and workshops bridging the gap between medical technology and alternative healing, suggests that we create a silent sanctuary in our homes and spend at least fifteen minutes a day there. If you think to yourself, "Oh sure, how am I going to do that in *my* house?" then you are just the person who needs to do this.

A silent retreat, whether organized or done on your own, in the manner of a Vision Quest, gives us another opportunity to be contemplative. In such retreats, hundreds of people sit in class or eat their meals together, and yet no one speaks. On the pathways, they do not talk or even look at each other. They do this so they may stay aware of each bite of food, each rise and fall of the feet. If you try silence, even for a day, you may discover whole worlds inside yourself.

You do not need to attend a long retreat to experience such inner awareness. Silence is a universal tool, found in all traditions. There is a quality in us that goes far beyond what we recognize as our individual personality. Silence is one of several ways we can reach those deep places of truth.

If you wish to use silence in your own ritual you might want to begin and end with a special sound. Once again, you can use a bell, or a single beat on a drum. This separates the silent time from the ordinary flow. Sit by your altar, or before some object that symbolizes your quest—perhaps a statue, a painting, a candle, or a simple stone. Ring the bell or hit the drum, and as the reverberations die down, follow them into silence. Let yourself sink into it, deeper with each breath. If focusing on your symbol helps you stay in touch, keep your eyes open. Otherwise, close them. As mental noise fills your mind (as it almost certainly will), just let your breath release it and return to silence. When you wish to finish, allow yourself to ring the bell from within the silence. Let its vibrations act like the divine voice re-creating the outer world. You can use this silence in a group, with one person taking the responsibility to begin and end the session. Such a person needs to feel the shape and texture of the group's silence in order to know when to end. This sounds paradoxical, but it may surprise you what becomes possible when you step out of the noise.

Chanting

Chanting may seem exotic to those of us from a secular or traditional Church background of sermons and hymns. We may think of chants as the mantras people were given in transcendental meditation—short phrases in a foreign lan-

The Sound of Many Hands Clapping

Rhythm is one of the greatest aids to entering a ritual state. We do not need instruments to experience its power. Our own hands, hitting each other or other parts of the body, such as the abdomen, can transport us to other worlds of consciousness. In flamenco, the passionate Gypsy music whose roots go back to Jewish and Islamic prayer, the earliest instrument was not the guitar or even the castanets, but the hands, still considered an instrument in their own right.

Some years ago, it occurred to archaeologists that the prehistoric caves might have been more than just a visual feast. They went through the chambers of Lascaux, clapping their hands. To their amazement, they discovered that the places where the sound reverberated most powerfully were exactly those places with the most intense paintings. Lascaux was the world's first multimedia performance space.

guage for people to say silently over and over in order to keep their minds from wandering during meditation. Or we might know only the Buddhist chant, "Om Mane Padme Aum," sometimes translated as "the jewel in the lotus." In fact, chanting is found in many traditions. Chanting is natural; it is one of those things children do spontaneously, and then "grow out of" if society does not encourage them to develop it in a more complex way. I remember doing this as a child, making up a simple melody and pouring out streams of syllables. It felt very free and exciting, as if the sounds belonged to a mysterious language from another world.

Sufi master Pir Vilayat Khan describes how the Sufis will chant "La iilha ha illa llah hu" for forty days, from morning to night. Anyone who does this, he says, cannot help but be transformed. In Wicca, there are the chants of the myriad names of the goddess from around the world. These are chosen not just for their qualities but for the rhythm of their repetition. All these chants have the triple quality of meaning, rhythm, and pure sound. They act directly on our bodies and yet they engage the mind through the statements they make.

None of the statements we chant represents absolute truth. They do represent different ways to approach the divine. The Muslim "There is no God save God" is one way of approaching the sacred. To chant the goddess names, "Hecate, Athena, Oya, Astarte, Nana, Inanna, Shekinah, Diana," approaches the sacred mystery from a different direction. We might think of the famous parable of the blind men and the elephant (the Sufi version of this tale describes the blind men as scholars, for the Sufis often stress the limitations of rigid intellectual approaches to religion). Three men, all blind, investigate an elephant. One touches the trunk and declares, "The elephant is a kind of snake." Another touches the side and pronounces, "An elephant is a wall." The third touches the foot and says, "The elephant is a tree." The simple meaning of this story is that people who believe they know the divine are blind fools. But there is a deeper level. Even if the blind men get only a partial sense of the elephant, they still have touched it, they still experience it. Before the sacred we are all blind, and any way we touch it, especially in ritual, will affect our lives.

So choose a chant that is meaningful to you. It may come from a recognized religious tradition, or it may be a line from a poem. Or it may be one you create yourself. If you have children, they might enjoy playing with the different possibilities to help you put together your chant, and then do it with you.

When you have chosen or created your chant, try it for several days. Repeat it, say it out loud, drum to it, experiment with the sounds and the rhythm, visualize the images, ponder the actual meaning of names or statements. Chant it in meditation, or in a dance. Use it in rituals, alone or with a group.

The Drum

The drum is the oldest musical instrument. In the Stone Age cave of Pêch-Mèrle, in France, whose vivid paintings go back more than twenty thousand years, archaeologists found a flat open area with crowded women's footsteps in all directions, as if from dancing. Against the wall they discovered a large flattened stone in the shape of a disk, and a stone club. When they struck the disk with the club, a drumbeat sounded off the cave walls. I have visited the cave, and seen and heard the drum. The sound is vibrant and alive.

One explanation for the drum's ancient and universal appeal is the way it mimics the human heartbeat. Feel your heart and you will recognize the thump of a drum. Rhythmic sound goes back to a time even before birth. Scientists have discovered that the womb is not silent. A fetus floating in the sea of its mother's belly will hear filtered noises from outside. Most of all, however, it hears the steady drumbeat of the heart that gives it life. Layne Redmond, who has studied the drum for many years, comments that it is not actually the mother's heart that the baby hears but the pulse of the blood as it surges through the arteries. When we hear the drum we unconsciously return to our oneness with our mothers, not just the individual woman we came to know but the beat of all life.

In her workshops and classes, and in her book *When the Drummers Were Women*, Redmond stresses the importance of art as ritual. Early in her career she was doing performance art but left it because of its artificiality. When a friend invited her to a Tibetan Buddhist four-day retreat and she heard monks perform traditional music, she was amazed. Art, she realized, needs to follow the basics of ritual. It needs to mark the seasons and rhythms of life, to take initiates through passages of death and rebirth.

For Redmond, the great breakthrough of her life came when she began to research the frame drum. These are handheld drums made by stretching an animal skin over a round wooden frame. The drummer holds the frame with one hand and strikes the surface with the other. Because you do not have to sit before a stationary floor drum, you can dance at the same time. Redmond discovered that almost all of the ancient pictures showed women as the drummers. Sometimes the women were priestesses to a goddess; sometimes a goddess herself played the drum.

Redmond formed the Mob of Angels, an all-female group devoted to ritual and performance with the frame drum. She deliberately slowed down the rhythm so that the beat would resonate with the women's own hearts. This gave their work a deep ceremonial quality. She began to explore the different rhythms for rituals of the Winter and Summer Solstices, the Fall and Spring Equinoxes. These are times when the Earth shifts and our bodies respond in subtle yet very different ways.

A Long Tradition

In an article in the June 1997 edition of *Percussion Notes* magazine, Redmond describes a bull ritual she attended in Brazil. Called *Bumba Meu Boi* (bumba is the sound of the drum, *meu* is "my," and *boi* is "bull"), it goes on every night for two months. Groups of people create elaborate beaded papier-mâché bulls, decorated with images of Christian saints, Adam and Eve, the Virgin Mary, and the African gods, especially the sea goddess Jemanja. Aphrodite, too, was a sea goddess, and "Mary" means "salt seas." To the sound of frame drums and musical bows, and with the spur of grain alcohol from a special chalice, the people ritually tear apart the bull and distribute the pieces for luck in the coming year.

Redmond compares this Bumba Meu Boi to an eight-thousand-year-old painting found in what may be the world's oldest city, uncovered near Çatal Hüyük, Turkey. There, thirty figures with instruments, including frame drums and musical bows, dance around an enormous bull.

We can go back even farther. That stone disk found in Pêch-Mèrle resembles nothing so much as a large frame drum. Lascaux is filled with images of bulls. And in another French cave, called Les Trois Frères, we find a painting of a shaman-like figure. Upright like a man, he has an animal head, as if he wears a mask. And he holds a musical bow.

The great power of ritual is exactly that it returns us to our deepest roots. We discover that the things that move us are the same things that moved our ancestors.

Music in Your Own Rituals

You do not need to train for years as a musician to use music in your own rituals. While a class will certainly help, you can find a drum and follow your own rhythms. If you have a frame drum, try standing in silence for several moments, following your breath and becoming aware of your heartbeat. In your mind, call upon the thousands of years of history of people using this instrument, and when you strike it think of the cave rituals, and the ancient initiations, and the great pulse of the waves. Do it slowly at first, for that solemn sense of ceremony, but then let it pick up speed on its own as your body sways to the sound.

In the last few years, many people have started drum groups, sometimes all men or all women. These groups allow their members to create a bond of primal sound, beyond words. The sessions usually take on a ritual power as the steady thunder of the drums lifts people beyond their normal consciousness.

There are other instruments well suited to ritual. As we will see next in chapter 6, a rattle, when used in a steady rhythm, can create a trancelike effect. Another useful—and very simple—instrument is the rainstick. This is a wooden tube filled with pebbles that move slowly down the tube when

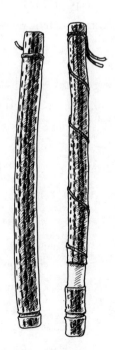

Rainsticks

you turn it end over end. Created in South America, the sticks mimic the sound of rain falling in the Amazon forests. Slowly turning a rainstick and letting the "rain" fall softly produces a deep, calming effect.

Another instrument that allows us to play on many levels is the five-note flute, or whistle. These are flutes based on cultures and traditions where the scale has no half notes (the *fa* and the *ti* in the Western scale). This makes them easy to improvise a simple melody. You can continue to discover tunes, or you can find a series of notes you like and repeat them over and over in the manner of a chant. If while you do this you visualize a particular god or goddess, the song will become your personal connection to that deity.

You also can use tapes and CDs to enhance your ritual work at home. There are records of drums from many traditions, chants that allow you to follow along as you sit before a candle or your altar, and recorded sounds from nature. The sound of the ocean can help settle us into a deeply contemplative state. So can the plaintive sound of whales calling to each other through the water. Recorded sounds of birds and other creatures from the Amazon rain forest help return us to the ancient memory of rituals in the intensity of nature.

Sight and sound are the senses that establish the environment and actions of ritual. The chants, the drums, the bells all help us go deeply into that special world. The other senses must also be present, however. As we will see in the next chapter, smell and taste allow us to enter the real physicality of ritual.

RESOURCES

Campbell, Don. *The Mozart Effect*. New York: Avon, 1997. (Accompanying CDs available from Spring Hill Music 303–938–1188).

Gass, Robert and Kathleen Brehony. *Chanting: Discovering Spirit in Sound*. New York: Broadway Books, 1999.

Greer, Mary K. *Tarot for Yourself*. Van Nuys, Calif.: Newcastle, 1984.

Hart, Mickey and Frederic Lieberman. *Planet Drum*. San Francisco: Harper/SanFrancisco, 1991.

Redmond, Layne. *When the Drummers Were Women.* New York: Crown, 1997.

Weil, Andrew, M.D. *Spontaneous Healing, Reprint Edition.* New York: Ballantine, 1996.

AUDIO PROGRAMS

Campbell, Don. *Healing Powers of Tone and Chant.* Theosophical Publishing House, 1994.

Gardner, Kay. *Music as Medicine.* Sounds True Audio.

Kabir, Chaitanya. *Divine Singing: How to Chant in the Devotional Tradition of India.* Sounds True Audio.

ANY MUSIC THAT IS MEANINGFUL TO YOU CAN BE USED IN RITUAL. THE FOLLOWING CD SAMPLER IS A TASTE OF THE MANY VARIETIES OF RITUAL AND WORLD MUSIC AVAILABLE

Dass, Krishna. *Pilgrim Heart.*

Gass, Robert. *Chant: The Best of World Chant.* Spring Hill Music (303–938–1188).

Gypsy Passion: New Flamenco. Narada (narada.com). Narada offers a wide selection of world sacred music.

Jilala: Sufi Trance Music from Morocco. Mystic Fire (800–292–9001).

Ni Riain, Noirin. *Celtic Soul.*

Redmond, Layne. *Being in Rhythm.*

Rhythms of the Goddess: Sacred Sounds of Santeria Ii. Inner Traditions.

Shankar, Ravi. *Chants of India.* Angel Records.

Many selections of sacred world music are available from Sounds True (800–333–9185), web site www.soundstrue.com.

Mickey Hart's Rykodisc label (rykodisc.com) in conjunction with the Library of Congress' Archive of Folk Culture has produced the series "Endangered Music Project," including sacred gamelan from Indonesia and music from the rain forests of South America and the Caribbean.

Also:

Hart, Mickey. *Planet Drum.* Rykodisc.

Olatunji, Babatunde. *Drums of Passion: The Beat.* Rykodisc/Mickey Hart Series.

VIDEOS

Drumming videos of Layne Redmond and Babatunde Olatunji available from Interworld Music and Video, see www.cnh.mv.net/ipusers/benj/video.html.

INSTRUMENTS

Blessings (323–930–2803) for Tibetan crystal bowls.

Cedar Mountain Drums (503–235–6345), mail order source for drums, flutes, and rattles.

Dharma Crafts (800–794–9862) for bells and gongs.

Taos Drums (800–424–DRUM).

Shaman's Drum magazine contains ads for many mail order instruments (541–552–0839).

5.

Smell and Taste

Even before you enter the room you smell the pungent sage. Inside the doorway, the leader of the ceremony moves the smudge stick around your body. Cleansed, you take your place in the circle.

The swirls of smoke rise up from the incense to the serene face of the golden Buddha. At his feet, in between the incense sticks, lies a small bowl of oranges.

The celebrants kneel and open their mouths to receive the wafer. As it touches the tongue they know that not only are they receiving the body of their Savior directly into their own bodies, they are joining an unbroken line of ritual that goes back to the Anointed One's own gift to his disciples.

The Witches have raised and released the cone of power. They have danced with fire and blessed each other with the goddess's abundance. And now it is time to feast! Salads and grains emerge, along with fruit juice and wine—and a large cake baked in the shape of a pregnant goddess.

Sense and Emotion

Smell and taste are the most immediate of senses. When we look at a sacred image, we automatically try to understand its meaning and origin. When we hear a chant, or a drum, we categorize the kind of sound it is, even as our bodies respond to the rhythm or melody. When we smell and taste, we bypass all that and experience the moment.

Food and scent are important in ritual partly because of their power to trigger memories. We all know how certain smells, especially of food, remind us of moments from years before. For many people, part of the joy of Christmas dinner is the way the smells conjure memories of Christmases as a child. Think of aromas that bring back memories for you. Did your mother wear a special perfume for parties? Did your grandmother bake a special cake for your birthday?

Smell and taste are bound up with our memories and emotions. You may always remember what you ate on your first date with your husband or wife. The smell of chicken soup on the stove may instantly transport you back to Grandma's house. When we attach particular foods to ritual traditions, we give the ritual a sense of familiarity and comfort. If we think back a moment to secular rituals, turkey and stuffing are part of the very soul of Thanksgiving. The purpose and meaning of the holiday is the need to express gratitude for the good things in life. We do this through special foods.

Since food is what keeps us alive, when we include it in ritual we celebrate our bodies and our presence in the world. By eating special foods, we form links with the past.

Cornucopia

We often associate certain foods with religious holidays, even when they are not officially part of the festival. Hot cross buns remind people of Easter. Roast goose may recall Christmas. Many Catholics still eat fish on Fridays.

Jewish tradition links particular foods with almost every festival. Sometimes, as in the Passover seder, the food is part of the ritual. More often it's a cultural tradition, but no less important in people's sense of ritual. For

Food and the New Year

When a year ends and another begins, we reaffirm our existence and express hope for the future. Because food is so basic, people all over the world use it ritually at the New Year. Here are some customs that you may want to adopt as part of a New Year's ritual.

In the United States, people drink champagne at the exact moment on television that the ball drops in Times Square. Champagne, already a ritual symbol of celebration, suggests optimism that the New Year will be cause to celebrate. African-Americans eat black-eyed peas on New Year's Day as a ritual for prosperity.

In China, people eat a whole range of symbolic foods for the Lunar New Year, which takes place around the end of January. They eat watermelon seeds to grow sweetness in their lives. At banquets, they serve a whole fish for prosperity, because of the abundant eggs fish lay. One of my own favorite customs involves the "kitchen god" that many Chinese people keep in their kitchens. The god is said to ascend to heaven on New Year's Day to report on the household. To make sure he gives a sweet account, Chinese families smear his lips with molasses!

Such New Year food rituals are closer to secular customs than full ritual. We can, however, make them part of a larger ritual for the turning of the year, or, in fact, any major transition.

Chanukah, nothing in the religion requires people to eat potato pancakes, but for Jews of European descent *latkes* are as vital as the candles they light each night of the festival.

Bread and Wine

The foods we use in ritual are often the most basic. Fruit is special because it is sweet and because it requires no cooking. This makes it a direct gift from the

Earth. The most common ritual foods, however, are two substances that people have to create from nature's raw materials—bread and wine.

What makes these two so special? Both have a transformative quality that makes them powerful in ritual. Bread is probably one of humanity's oldest inventions. We take various substances, mix them into a gooey paste, and then bake them in a dark hot oven, making something wholesome and delicious. If the baking of bread symbolizes birth, fermentation represents death and resurrection. Through a mysterious process very close to decay, raw plants emerge as a mind-altering drink.

We know of these famous foods from the Christian mass. Tom F. Driver, author of *The Magic of Ritual*, hopes to restore the importance of meaningful ritual to Christianity. Driver describes a service he attended when the bread and wine were passed from person to person in a mood of great joy, rather than the "funereal" tones Driver has found in many modern churches.

We know of bread and wine also from the Jewish blessing that was Christ's inspiration for the mass. Jews actually use bread and wine at virtually every special occasion, not just the Passover meal that formed the Christian Last Supper. After a religious service, or before the Sabbath dinner, Jews will say a blessing over wine with a special prayer, and then a separate blessing over bread. Some contemporary synagogues make this a communal ritual by having everyone touch the *challah* (special bread for the Sabbath and other holidays), or touch someone who is touching the challah, or someone who is touching someone. . . . All the while, everyone chants together the blessing. Afterward, the bread can be shared among everyone. This practice can be done with any food as a powerful way to bind people together.

The symbolism of bread and wine goes back thousands of years. Eight-thousand-year-old Turkish ruins revealed ovens for baking bread, and on top of each oven was a figure of a pregnant goddess. Did Stone Age people associate the miraculous transformation of raw dough into bread with the creation of a baby in a woman's body? That same association exists today when we say that a pregnant woman has "a bun in the oven."

In many ancient cultures a god of grain was also the inventor of wine and the bringer of civilization. The ancient Egyptians taught that the goddess Isis discovered barley and her husband Osiris discovered first how to cultivate it and then how to ferment it into wine. Together, they taught the rule of law to the Egyptians and then the world. Osiris, colored green in paintings, symbolized the grain that died each year in the drought and returned to life with the annual flood of the Nile. In Greece, Dionysius, described as the inventor of wine, was also said to travel the world and teach civilization to primitive humanity. The myths of both Osiris and Dionysius include dismemberment—the harvesting of the grain—and return to life—the sprouting of new seeds. And of course, Jesus, too, is killed and returns to life.

Wine in ritual can present problems for some people. Because our culture sees alcohol as amusement, some people become addicted. In recovery they need to avoid even the taste. For this reason, some churches and ritual groups offer grape juice as an alternative.

How to Use Wine in Ritual

If you do feel comfortable using wine, treat it with the respect it deserves as one of humanity's oldest symbolic foods. Keep a special cup or chalice just for ritual use. There are many beautiful silver or crystal chalices in gift shops and religious supply stores.

The particular wine should also be only for ceremonies. You might want to do a small ritual or blessing when you first open the bottle. Before anyone drinks from the chalice, pour some on the ground (if outside) or in a bowl for an offering. Here is a sample blessing: "As this wine pours freely, let our lives flow with joy. Let the magic of this wine help us recognize the magic of transformation in our own lives."

Ritual solemnity does not have to mean stuffiness. You can dance with the wine, you can enjoy the taste of it and the sense of celebration. You do not have to get drunk to recognize wine's ecstatic symbolism.

If the ritual is for a small group of people, recork the bottle and set it aside for further ceremonial use. By making it unique in this way, we acknowledge that we drink it for more than intoxication.

Goddess Cookery

Just as you enjoy the wine of ritual, so you can play with the whole sacred use of food. If your ritual includes a feast, you might want to prepare the food with your children. Using an herbalism guide, you and your family can gather wild plants. You can bake breads and cakes in various shapes, either of gods or goddesses, or of symbolic objects. All these preparations increase the excitement and meaning of the ritual itself.

Cait Johnson, in her book *Cooking Like a Goddess,* describes the many ways we can restore the sacredness of food and its preparation. She reminds us that we are all "connected to our mother planet and the food she gives us, but many of us have forgotten the connection is a sacred one." The high prevalence of eating disorders in recent years, from anorexia to compulsive overeating, suggests to Johnson that our very souls are hungry. When we use food and cooking in ritual, we feed our souls as well as our bodies.

The Sacred Kitchen

To restore sacredness to food, Cait Johnson suggests first of all that we create a special place in the kitchen just for ourselves. This "power place" can be as simple as a comfortable chair that the whole family knows belongs to you alone.

She goes on to suggest that you create an altar in your kitchen. A small statue or painting of one or more favorite goddesses could serve as the center. Some examples of kitchen goddesses might include the "Venus of Willendorf" (the thirty-thousand-year-old figurine found in Austria), or the Greek goddesses Demeter (grain) and Hestia (hearth). Johnson focuses exclusively on goddesses. Some people might wish to include such grain and wine figures as Osiris and Dionysius.

You can mount a painting or photo of a sacred image on cardboard, or, of course, frame it. You also could make your own figure with Sculpey or papier-mâché.

Change your altar from time to time. Set one of the goddesses outside for a while (perhaps by your tree shrine—see chapter 3), and then bring her back to the kitchen.

Your kitchen altar should include some aspect of you, maybe a symbol of your career or hobbies, or a favorite memento. Do a ritual to consecrate your altar. Inhale deeply, look about the kitchen, and exhale. Then say a short blessing before the altar. You also might sprinkle salt and water about the edges, burn incense or a smudge stick, or read a poem or a traditional blessing.

You can extend the ritual with a special meal designed to honor a deity on your altar. This could include food from the original culture, such as stuffed grape leaves for Greek goddesses. Cait Johnson calls such meals "Kitchen Goddess Feasts."

A similar meal is an "ancestor feast," designed to honor your family's roots. Include favorite recipes of a grandparent, or the dishes from your ethnic heritage. Before the meal, light a candle in tribute to the ancestors. While you eat, invite everyone to tell stories of relatives or cultural history.

When you do a meal as a ritual, set aside a small amount of the food you prepare as an offering. You can scatter some bits on your altar (perhaps in a small decorated jar if you worry about attracting insects), or, if you live in the country, put out a small amount of the best dish for local birds and other animals.

Food as Symbolism

Knowing the symbolic meanings of food—symbolism that often goes back many thousands of years—can give the simplest meal a special sacred dimension. For example, the biblical phrase "land flowing with milk and honey" means a land of prosperity and joy. Have you ever wondered about the source of this expression? It goes back to Near Eastern goddesses and beyond, all the way to the Stone Age. Milk and honey come from cows and bees, two animals associated with goddesses, not just in the Mediterranean area but all over the world. The bee symbolizes the benevolent goddess because

Sacred cow

of the sweet honey, and because the queen bee seems the very model of a nurturing goddess and her worshipers. Artemis, one of the oldest of the Greek goddesses, was called "Melissa," or bee, and was sometimes depicted as half woman, half bee. Stone Age tombs were built in the shape of a beehive as a symbol of rebirth.

The association of cows with primordial goddesses is almost universal. In Egypt we find Hathor the cow goddess, the oldest known deity. The Greeks believed the Milky Way (our galaxy) streamed from the teats of a cow goddess. The Lakota Indians speak of White Buffalo Woman, the giver of the Pipe. Africa has Oya, a buffalo goddess. In Scandinavian mythology, an immortal cow shaped the world

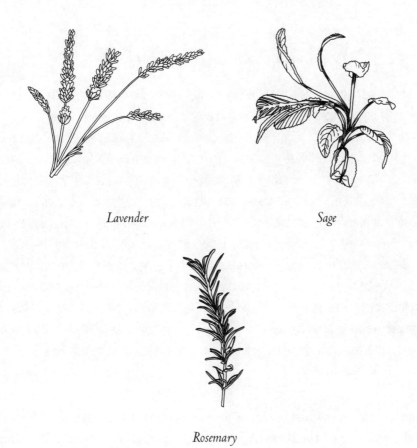

Lavender

Sage

Rosemary

from a block of ice. The "holy cows" of India are so sacred to this day that no one may harm them. And in Lascaux and the other caves, pregnant cows appear alongside their mighty consorts, the bulls. The cow is universal partly because her milk resembles that of women, partly because the curved horns suggest the crescent Moons, and partly because her massive size and placidity give her a quiet strength.

Ritual Meals

The Passover seder, a celebration of the Jews' liberation from slavery, is the perfect example of a ritual meal. Every food symbolizes an event, or quality, in the story.

A Ritual for Milk and Honey

Just as bread and wine celebrate the dying and resurrecting god, so a simple ritual with milk and honey honors the Mother, who is ever with us, ancient and undying.

Here are a couple of suggestions. You can, of course, make up your own. Pour milk into a small ornate bowl. Take it outside on a clear night and hold it up high, as an offering to the Milky Way of stars. Say a simple blessing, such as "We [I, if you are alone] honor the goddess, older than knowledge, whose milk of love and nourishment flows through our lives." Sip from the bowl as if from a sacramental chalice. If you do this ritual in the country or in a park, you can leave the milk outside for the animals.

Set out a dish of honey (if possible, organic honey from a small farm, rather than a factory). Cut an apple across the middle. If there is a group, show everyone the perfect five-pointed star that will appear in each half. Then cut the apple into a piece for each person. After each has dipped the piece in the honey, say, "We honor the goddess, forever alive, who brings sweetness, beauty, and wonder into our lives."

For example, the unleavened bread, or *matzo*, represents the "bread of affliction"—that is, the suffering of the slaves. At the same time, it also represents liberation, for the story tells us that the people had to leave Egypt so quickly they could not wait to leaven their bread. Every action has a ritual meaning. The guests dip an egg in salt water to signify new life in the midst of tears.

As a meal, it involves the whole family. The seder formally begins when the youngest asks four questions around the theme "Why is this night different from all other nights?"

The entire eight-day holiday of Passover revolves around food. To set aside Passover, Jews not only avoid certain foods—regular bread and cake, legumes, and others—but also use entirely separate dishes, silverware, and pots and pans. The ritual begins the afternoon of the first evening with a ceremony children love. Armed with a candle, for light in dark corners, and a feather, for thoroughness, the parents and children "search" the house for bread crumbs. Once they have purified the house in this way, they can begin to prepare the meal.

In recent years, Jews have sought ways to bring renewed meaning to the holiday, reflective of modern life. One way involves a focus on the theme of liberation. Rabbi Martha Houseman creates what she calls a "freedom plate" alongside the traditional plate of symbolic food. Everyone brings some object that has symbolized freedom for them in the past year. They put these things on the plate and speak about them in turn.

A very different kind of ritual meal is the Japanese Tea Ceremony. In simplest terms, the Tea Ceremony involves serving tea and sweets to guests. The Zen masters believe this simplicity can serve as a model for all of life. The ceremony can last up to five hours, which includes the preparation of the food, an integral part of the ritual.

Because the ceremony varies with the seasons, it joins you to nature. Because you cannot do it alone—you must pour the tea for guests—it teaches relationships. Because it requires a beautiful scroll, it increases your appreciation for art. The Tea Ceremony also trains you in awareness of flower arrangement, bamboo carving, calligraphy, pottery, religious philosophy, meditation, food preparation, cleanliness, and service to others.

Four aspects come together in the Tea Ceremony: *wa,* "harmony"; *kei,* "respect"; *sei,* "purity"; and *jaku,* "tranquillity." We learn harmony because the Tea Ceremony requires that all aspects function together. You cannot just go at the last minute, after work, and pick up the sweet you want to serve. You must prepare it with kei for all the ingredients and effort that go into creating it. Even the plates receive honor and ritual bows. The lesson of sei—purity—comes as you ritually purify the implements and the settings over and over. The tranquillity of jaku comes as you learn to perform every action, from pouring tea to eating to washing the dishes, with attention and care.

All these things become ritual through the Zen quality of mindfulness, the ability to focus all attention on what you are doing. If you do a rite of your own that includes food, try to do it with a sense of devotion and service, from the shopping to the cleaning up. Such mindfulness will make the experience much deeper, for yourself and for the people who join you in the meal.

Fasting

Just as silence can be a ritual sound, so a fast forms part of the spiritual approach to food. Fasting as a way to approach the sacred is practiced in different ways across the world. Native American teacher Ed McGaa describes how someone on a Vision Quest goes without food or water. To enter the world of the gods, Siberian shamans will sometimes go into the ice without food for days.

Fasting is not a punishment or a penance. It is an opening, but it only really works when we do it with joy. Jews fast on the Day of Atonement in order to direct their whole attention to prayer. Some fasts are less strict than others, but may last longer. For example, Muslims fast from sunrise to sunset for the entire month of Ramadan. During those hours they must not eat or drink, not even water. When the Sun goes down some eat heartily, but many keep their meals very simple. Catholics traditionally do not eat meat during Lent, the forty days that precede Easter. Many also vow to give up some additional pleasure or indulgence.

A sacred fast is very different from a diet, or even a medical fast to clear your body of toxic residues. In a sacred fast you do not simply deny yourself food. You shift your consciousness. During a sacred fast you use prayer, devotion, and mindfulness to turn away from negativity and ordinary day-to-day obsessions. During Ramadan, Muslims seek to abstain from anger, hatred, and hostility as much as food. To fast in this way can be a wonderful experience for all of us, whatever our religious background.

If you wish to try a ritual fast, set aside a time when you also can break from your ordinary daily activities. Make the fast part of some wider ritual activity, such as a Vision Quest in nature, or a day of celebration with others, or a retreat. That way you genuinely shift your awareness rather than spend the day with thoughts of how soon you can eat again. Eat a good meal the night before, and drink plenty of water (not soda or coffee, and definitely not alcohol, which will dehydrate you). Do not be too strict with yourself, especially the first time you try it. If you feel sick, or dizzy, take some food and water. (WARNING: If you have a medical condition, such as diabetes, that requires steady levels of blood sugar, do not attempt to fast. You also should not fast if you have just recovered from a serious illness.)

The flip side of the sacred fast is the feast. Notice how similar the two words are. In the world of ritual, extremes often mirror each other. In earlier times, Catholics preceded the abstentions of Lent with the Carnival. Since Lent always begins on Ash Wednesday, the day before became known as Fat Tuesday, or, in French, Mardi Gras. Thus, the extravagant parades in New Orleans originally derived from the fast that followed them.

Just as a sacred fast is more than denial of food, so a sacred feast is not just a wild party. Carnivals go back thousands of years. The costumes and parades derive from processions and ecstatic dances in which people acted out the roles of the gods and goddesses. When Christianity replaced Paganism, the gods and goddesses stayed alive as the Carnival figures. In the Middle Ages, when the social order was highly stratified, the Carnival gave people a chance to break the rules and to experience life from a different perspective.

Your Own Carnival

If you belong to a ritual group, you might want to plan your own Carnival celebration. Two possible times are the Winter Solstice, when the world turns from darkness to light, and the Spring Equinox, when life is resurgent and the day and night are in magical balance.

Use costumes and masks so that you all have a chance to play with taking on the personalities of kings and queens, tricksters and warriors, magicians and fools. Have everyone bring their favorite dishes and treats. Plan to play music, especially music with drums and other percussion instruments.

Above all, enjoy yourself! Remember the Wiccan words of the goddess: "All acts of love and pleasure are my rituals."

The Power of Scent

The importance of food is obvious. Without food we cannot live. Scent is more subtle, and yet the popularity of aromatherapy demonstrates that scent can affect us in dramatic ways.

Essential oils are the pure distillation of natural substances, so powerful that just a few molecules in the air can produce strong reactions. Perfumes, by comparison, are mixtures of several things, including chemicals.

We tend to underestimate the importance of smell. We actually have more brain tissue devoted to this sense than any other. The olfactory nerve is connected to the oldest part of our brains (going back before mammals), the limbic system. Smell touches us in a place of deep instincts. According to Mary Greer, author of *The Essence of Magic*, our brains actually grow from the olfactory stalks. She quotes Diane Ackerman, author of *The Natural History of the Senses:* "We think because we smell."

All of this makes oils and incense and other scents invaluable for ritual.

A Brief History of the Use of Scent in Ritual

Tracing the history of scent's connection to ceremonies and magic will give us an idea of just how valuable it can be in ritual. The earliest known use of scent in rituals was as incense burned to attract the gods and keep away demons. This was more important than personal attractiveness, or covering up bad odors. During the ceremony, people would throw leaves, twigs, and needles onto the fire, both to keep the flames alive and as offerings to the spirits.

Many countries recognized the importance of incense and other aromas. In Egypt, Hatshepsut, a woman who ruled as Pharaoh, traded with neighboring lands for frankincense and myrrh, the same substances (along with gold) that the

Magi—magicians—bring to the infant Jesus in the manger. Some 1,450 years after Hatshepsut, Cleopatra, famed as a sorceress, covered her sails with scented oils so that all along the Nile people would know that a goddess was sailing past them.

The Greeks believed in a divine origin for all aromatic plants. The priestesses of the great oracle at Delphi anointed themselves with oils and leaned over burning bay leaves so that the smoke would induce visions. Priestesses of ritual prophecy have followed similar practices in places as diverse as India, Africa, Java, and South America.

India knew the practice of distilling oils at least as early as 3000 B.C.E. The Indians used sandalwood, both to induce calm and to repel termites! Later, the sexual rites of Tantra developed complex uses of oils and incense for both men and women.

Scent came to Europe from the Arab lands, via the Crusaders. The term "rosary" derives from the fact that people originally made the beads from crushed rose petals that released their fragrance when their owners fingered them. Devotees of Mary consider the rose her flower. Earlier, the Greeks pictured Aphrodite lying on roses to receive her lovers, from which we get the expression "bed of roses," and from which arose the idea of a gift of roses as an expression of love. Every time we give roses to a romantic partner, we are reenacting an ancient ritual.

Use of Essential Oils

You can use both incense and oils in various ways to enhance your rituals. Scent helps create the ritual space as it fills the atmosphere of the room. You can use a few drops of oil in a bath before the ritual to purify yourself, or anoint yourself with a diluted mixture. If you use essential oils as part of a ritual, it can have a cumulative effect. Each time you use a particular scent at a certain point, it will reinforce the experience for the next time. After a while, the scent alone can bring back the feeling of the ritual.

Essential Oils, Aromatherapy, and Ritual

The practice of aromatherapy recognizes that particular scents bring out special qualities. While you can use these strictly for healing, you also can use them in ritual to develop those qualities. Here are some examples, taken from *Aromatherapy: Scent and Psyche,* by Peter and Kate Damian:

Bay leaves	Clarify, relax, help respiration
Bergamot	Calms, refreshes, helps anxiety
Cardamom	Stimulates, brightens
Cinnamon	Antiseptic, warms and stimulates
Eucalyptus leaves	Antiinflammatory, soothe
Fennel	Strengthens, encourages
Grapefruit peel	Refreshes, uplifts
Jasmine leaves	Euphoric, antidepressant
Lemon peel	Refreshes, revivifies, increases circulation
Patchouli	Arouses, aphrodisiac
Pine needles	Strengthen, stabilize
Spearmint	Invigorates, refreshes
Yarrow leaves	Calm, balance, soothe

Ways to Use Essential Oils

There are several methods to bring out the scent from essential oils. Use pure oils and not synthetics, and always dilute the oils with a carrier, such as ordinary massage oil or vegetable oil, or water. Diluted in water, you can spray the scent in the air. Fara Shaw Kelsey, an herbalist and healer, uses a few drops of thyme in a bottle of water to purify the air. Thyme has powerful antiseptic qualities.

Essential oils are very strong, and you should avoid undiluted contact with the skin. Only a few are actual irritants, but if you get a rash or feel a burning sensation, wash the area with cold water and apply plain vegetable oil. Never use them internally or on the mucous membranes.

As well as spraying diluted oils in the air, or pouring a few drops in a bath, you can diffuse essential oils with heat. Many stores now sell aroma lamps or ceramic rings that fit onto lightbulbs. These will warm a small amount of oil and release the molecules into the air. In winter you can place a few drops in water in a ceramic bowl and place it on a heater. As the water evaporates, it carries the scent into the air. Two drops of essential oil in $1/4$ to $1/2$ cup of distilled water will work for a small room, six to ten drops for a larger space. Make sure the water doesn't boil. There also are electric diffusers that will spray the air with molecules from pure essential oils.

Smudge Sticks and Cornmeal

American Indians have always used both scent and food in ritual. Today, non-Indians have adopted many of these practices, both for their actual effects and for the link to an ancient tradition that honors the Earth. When we cast grains in the air, or set out bits of food, or pour a few drops of wine or juice on the ground, we symbolically offer ourselves to the powers that sustain our lives. When Indians gather herbs for healing rituals, they always make sure not to take the entire plant. Then they thank it and leave something behind, such as cornmeal or tobacco. This exchange acknowledges that the Earth and its creatures do not exist solely for our benefit. Many modern herbalists, who often "wildcraft"—that is, pick wild plants to make their medicines—follow the Indian practice. You might want to gather your own edible plants for the feast part of your ritual, or for an offering. There are many books on herbalism that will identify the abundance of wild food that exists even in urban parks. A local herbalist will sometimes give "weed walks," where he or she takes you around an area and points out the many wild plants with medicinal or nutritional value. You will be amazed at the incredible abundance growing all around us.

One Native American custom followed by many non-Indians is the smudge stick. This is a tied bundle of some fragrant dried plant, most commonly sage. When lit by a match, it gives off pungent smoke. You can wave the stick about the room to purify the air for the start of a ritual. Many people also use it to cleanse themselves and others, especially in a group ritual. You can find smudge sticks in many metaphysical or health food stores.

Tobacco and Ritual

A Native American practice that troubles some people is the use of tobacco. Because cigarettes have killed so many, we may find it hard to see tobacco as a sacred herb. There is, however, a great difference between commercial tobacco, chemically treated to increase addiction, and the small amounts of pure tobacco smoked in a Pipe Ceremony or simply scattered as an offering to the Earth. For many people, the smoke of the pipe, as it rises into the air and vanishes, becomes a pathway to the world of the Spirits. Still, anyone who has suffered from nicotine addiction may sensibly want to avoid any tobacco consumption at all. If such people find themselves in a Native American ritual that includes passing a pipe, they should simply pass it on when it comes to them. Some groups who wish to adapt the Pipe Ceremony in their own rituals substitute some natural, nonaddictive herb for tobacco. Many health food stores carry such herbs.

These are only a few of the many ways we use food and scent in ritual. As we have seen, some are solemn, some are playful. These two senses touch so many areas of our lives that their ritual possibilities are nearly endless. And yet the final sense, touch, is also vast, for it brings us to our very physical presence in the world, our bodies. In the next chapter, we will end our tour of the five senses with a look at the ways our bodies move and respond to the experiences of ritual.

RESOURCES

BOOKS

Ackerman, Diane. *A Natural History of the Senses, Reprint Edition.* New York: Vintage, 1991.

Brill, Steve with Evelyn Dean. *Identifying and Harvesting Edible and Medicinal Plants in Wild (And Not So Wild) Places.* New York: Hearst Books, 1994.

Damian, Peter and Kate. *Aromatherapy: Scent and Psyche.* Rochester, Vt.: Healing Arts Press, 1995.

Driver, Tom F. *The Magic of Ritual.* San Francisco: HarperSanFrancisco, 1991.

Greer, Mary K. *The Essence of Magic.* Van Nuys, Calif.: Newcastle, 1993.

Johnson, Cait. *Cooking Like a Goddess.* Rochester, Vt.: Healing Arts Press, 1997.

LeGuérer, Annick. *Scent: The Mysterious and Essential Powers of Smell, Reprint Edition.* New York: Kodansha, 1994.

Soshitsu, Sen XV. Translated by V. Dixon Morris. *The Japanese Way of Tea.* Honolulu: The University of Hawaii Press, 1998.

Wolfson, Ron. *The Art of Jewish Living: The Passover Seder.* Woodstock, Vt.: Jewish Lights, 1996.

Worwood, Valerie Ann. *The Complete Book of Essential Oils and Aromatherapy.* New York: New World Library, 1991.

MAIL ORDER HERBS AND SMUDGE STICKS
Cedar Mountain Drums (503–235–6345).

Blessings (323–930–2803) for herbal chakra pillows.

6.
Touch and
the Body

As you prepare for the Easter celebration, you take a long, luxurious shower. The water pouring down your body washes away your ordinary worries and concerns. You dress in clean clothes to symbolize new life, green in honor of Spring. You and your daughter put flowers in each other's hair. Now you are ready to go to church.

Everyone holds hands in the circle. Moonlight floods down from the skylight. As if to take the Moon itself and pass it around, someone squeezes the hand of the person next to her, who squeezes the hand of the person next to him, and so on around and around, received and given, faster and faster. Suddenly, with a low hum, all reach into the center and then, with a great shout, fling up their arms in a wild burst of joy.

The Importance of Touch

Like taste, touch in ritual is often involved with pleasure. We love the feel of fabrics and jewelry; we get a sense of strength from touching the Earth. Touch is fundamental to our sense of reality. Babies always want to touch things to make sure they exist.

In ritual, when we touch the objects we use, they become more real to us. We hold hands in a circle to establish the most basic energy link, one person connected to another. At the end of the ritual, we may hug our neighbor as a direct way to share the emotions we have experienced. Two bodies touching each other are more eloquent than any words.

Touch involves our whole bodies. The largest organ of the human body is the skin. If we just stand on a hill and feel the breeze, we are touching the air, touching the ground. When we dance, alone or with others, we allow our bodies to express things we could never describe or paint.

A Ritual for Touch

This ritual is best done with a small group of people who know and feel comfortable with each other. If possible, do it outdoors in a place where the participants can walk barefoot. If done in a room, choose one with a pleasant floor surface that you will not harm with a little water.

1. Prepare the ritual area or room by placing a cauldron or other large container in the center. Scatter soft flower petals around it so that as people go up to it they feel the petals under their feet. There should also be a bowl or pitcher of water large enough to pour some on each person's hands.

2. Everyone brings four objects: a long silk scarf; a rock; something soft (small stuffed animal toys are fine); and something smooth, such as a rounded polished stone or small carving.

3. One person agrees to act as leader. She (or he) arrives early and puts on layers of fabric of different textures over her clothes, one layer for each of the participants. The fabric can simply be draped over the shoulder or around the neck. At the beginning of the ritual the leader stands silently in front of the cauldron.

4. The participants enter one by one. The first lays the silk scarf at the leader's feet, places the other objects in the cauldron, and then removes one of the leader's fabrics and drapes it over the side of the cauldron. The others do the same, except that each one ties his or her silk scarf loosely to the end of the previous one, so that the scarves end up as a multicolored rope. As each removes a piece of fabric from the leader, she or he describes something to "uncover." They might say, "I uncover truth," or "I uncover memory," or "I uncover courage." Then they step back and take a place in a circle around the center. When they have found their place, they close their eyes.

5. When everyone has entered the circle, the leader walks over to them and joins their hands, saying, "Let all that you have uncovered join together."

6. The leader asks everyone to hold out their hands. They do so, hands cupped together to receive. The leader takes the bowl of water and pours a small amount on each person's hands, saying, "May you be cleansed of all worry and trouble."

7. Now the leader takes the tied silk scarves and winds them in and out of the people's arms, one scarf for each person, saying, "Let the gentleness of this cord symbolize the gentle firm ties that hold us together." The scarves should be loose enough for the people to bend down without pulling them loose.

8. The leader gives each person a rock, saying, "Let this rock reveal the strength within you." They all hold the rocks for a short time, then set them down.

9. The leader gives each one a soft object, saying, "May your life always have moments of softness and pleasure." They hold the objects for a time, then set them down.

10. The leader gives each one a smooth object, saying, "May your life flow smoothly, both in times of hardship and joy." They hold the objects for a time, then set them down.

11. The leader unties the scarves, leaving them draped on each person's arms or wrists, saying, "Walk freely and know that love ties us all together."

12. Eyes open, everyone bends down and touches the ground or floor. All say, "We draw strength from the Earth." Then all step forward to form a tighter circle around the leader, with everyone touching. The ritual ends as everyone says, "We give strength to each other."

The Sacred Body

The body is not just something we own, however much our language uses phrases like "my body." Nor is it a prison for the soul, or—the other extreme—an exalted temple. The body is simply our physical reality. We express ourselves through our bodies, and if we try to tell lies, to others or to ourselves, our body language speaks the truth. When we share our sexuality with each other, we share our deepest selves.

The body carries memories long after the conscious mind has tried to dismiss them. We may remember our past hurts or fears through a stiff neck or back pain. But the body also remembers our joy, and even in our darkest moments, we can recover our hopes, and our freedom, and our knowledge of sacred reality through the honest truth of our bodies. When we touch things of beauty, or dance, or hold hands during a chant, or bow or put our hands together in gestures of devotion, we reconnect to the wonder of life.

Dance as a Way to Truth

Anytime we move we express what we feel, even if we are not conscious of it. We move stiffly when afraid, jerkily when angry, with a spring in our steps when we're happy, sensuously when we feel sexy. Most of the time we are not aware of what we express with our bodies. By including different kinds of movements in our rituals, especially dance, we can awaken knowledge of ourselves and of sacred awareness.

Gabrielle Roth has performed and taught ecstatic dances for many years. According to Roth, any path to wholeness must begin in our bodies. She describes us as absentee landlords of our own bodies, out of touch with life. Through her study and work she has identified five rhythms she considers basic to all people, whatever their cultural background. These are Flow, a feminine rhythm; Staccato, a masculine rhythm; Chaos, for letting go; Lyrical, for celebration; and Stillness, for introspection. Together they make up what Roth calls "the Wave," a flow of movements that encompasses all of life. Both women and men experience all of the rhythms at different times and in different situations.

While we all have our own unique experiences, Roth points out that the arc of life is basically the same for all of us. We are born, we travel through childhood, puberty, and maturity, and then we die. Roth believes that each of the phases of life belongs to a teacher. The teacher for birth is the mother, for childhood the father, for puberty the self, for maturity society, and for death serenity and the universe. These phases and teachers go with the five rhythms. From birth/mother we learn the Flow, from childhood/father we get Staccato, from puberty and the self we experience the Chaos of letting go, in maturity we learn to celebrate with Lyric rhythm, and as we approach death we seek serenity in Stillness.

You can learn Gabrielle Roth's rhythms and dance in her CDs or her video, "The Wave." You also can explore such rhythms through your own movements, choosing music or simply sounds that inspire you to move and to learn.

Dances to Take You Outside Yourself

We have seen how the word "ecstasy" means to stand outside yourself—that is, outside your ego, with its criticism and separation from life. Throughout the world, people have used rhythmic dance to achieve this ecstatic state. In the thirteenth century the Persian poet and mystic Rumi (currently the number-one-selling poet in America!) began the so-called whirling dervishes, people who spin about with one foot in the center as their white clothes swirl out in orbit around their bodies. Through this practice, which dervishes can do for hours, they reach a state of oneness with the divine mystery of existence. Pir Vilayat Khan teaches this whirling tradition in his classes. With true Sufi eclecticism, he will use music such as Bach along with traditional Persian songs. The beauty of the music and the graceful repetition raise the spirit to states of joy.

Members of the Hasidic sect of Judaism also practice ecstatic dance. Hasidism features highly expressive melodies and free-form dancing, often with the arms out and the head back, as if to invite God to flow into your body.

Some of the first Christian groups also followed practices similar to those of the dervishes. They called it "round dancing." And in the nineteenth century the radical Christian group known as the Shakers rediscovered such movements. Their famous hymn "Simple Gifts" contains the lines "To turn, turn will be our delight / Till by turning, turning / We come round right."

Ecstatic Dance

You do not need to be a dervish or a Shaker to experience ecstatic dance.

1. Find a simple melody that you can keep in your head. You might listen to a CD of spiritual songs. Choose a song that stirs you deep inside. You can choose to memorize the words or simply hum the melody.

2. Go somewhere open and peaceful. If weather and environment permits, go to an open field (a rooftop works well in the city).

3. Stand loosely and remember the melody. Be aware of the beauty around you. Open your arms wide, lift your head, and breathe deeply.

4. Begin humming or singing. Begin very softly, then let it become as loud or quiet as it inspires you to.

5. When the melody takes you, begin to sway, to move, and then to dance.

6. Let yourself surrender to the movement like a river that will carry you joyously to the light.

Trance States Through Movement

When we think of going into a trance, we usually think of meditation. Dance is actually a much more common method for inducing trances. This is especially true for African cultures. In the religions of West Africa, and their American offshoots—Haitian Vodou, Mexican Santeria, Brazilian Candomblé—dance opens the way for specific gods and goddesses to take over a person's body in the controlled conditions of the communal ritual. In Haiti, where the Vodou tradition calls the gods *loas,* the dancers sometimes refer to themselves as "horses," to be ridden by whichever loa the drums have summoned. In a true Vodou ritual (compared to the ones staged for tourists), the drumming and dancing go on for hours. The dancers move with a steady repetition until one of the dancers begins to shake and fall backward, so that the other dancers have to support him or her. The person's whole manner changes, becoming more confident and powerful as "The Divine Horsemen," to use the title of a famous book on Vodou by Maya Deren, take over. For as much as an entire night the person will act the part of the loa. After a time, the loa leaves the person, who then returns to his or her normal perceptions and behavior.

Body Language

We use the term "body language" to describe unconscious movements or postures that reveal our emotions or state of mind. Some traditions, however, have created a literal language of movements and gestures. In Hindu dance every part of the body—the placement of the fingers, the turn of the feet, the lift of an eyebrow—says something precise in the tales of the gods and demons.

The Arabic tradition of belly dancing derives from similar, very ancient traditions. Most people think of belly dancing as seductive entertainment, but it originally expressed women's creative power and closeness to the Earth. Some modern

Your Own Ritual Performance

Vodou trance rituals are very powerful performances that belong specifically to that culture. However, if you wish to experience acting out the role of a god or goddess, you can use some of the methods of trance, but in a lighter, more playful way. Here are some suggestions.

Do this with a group. Choose a mythological character that interests you. Research the character's qualities and imagery, then lay out some of the clothing and symbolic objects that belong to the deity. You do not need elaborate costumes. Be creative. For example, if you wanted to invoke Yemanja, the West African *orisha* of the sea, you might lay out a flowing dress, a necklace of seashells, and a large bowl of salt water.

Choose a song or rhythm suitable to invoke this figure. You can have fun experimenting with different songs ahead of time. Try to choose one with a simple, steady rhythm. See the resource section at the end of chapter 4 or visit the world music section of a good record store to find examples of songs and chants dedicated to various gods and goddesses.

Begin the ritual with everyone in a circle around the objects and clothing you have chosen. Hold hands to create the physical link. Begin a quiet hum. As the energy builds and the hum becomes the song, someone calls out an invocation—for example, "We invoke Yemaja, orisha of the great waters." Dance with the song.

Wait for someone to feel the inspiration to act out the character. Others can play along, encouraging him or her. This performance does not have to be overly serious. Let yourself strut, or leap, or make faces. Sometimes a playful attitude, with everyone joining in, will actually carry the experience further than will attempts at grand gestures or poetry.

After some time, the energy will die down. The person can remove the costume and the circle can re-form. Everyone sings the song. The person who first invoked the character now thanks her or him. The song dies down to a hum and people release their hands.

women have begun to rediscover the practice as a way to get in touch with their own bodies. It also helps many women move away from the unrealistic media image of the supermodel to a greater appreciation of their own bodies.

You do not need to take on the religious beliefs behind either of these traditions to appreciate the new awareness they will give you of your body and all it can express. Why not try a class and see what you discover for yourself?

Postures and Trance Journeys

Just as dance can bring us to greater self-awareness, so the postures of the body can have a powerful effect.

Felicitas Goodman, author of *Where the Spirits Ride the Wind*, is an anthropologist who became interested in "glossolalia," the academic term for what Pentecostal Christians call "speaking in tongues," or, in other words, the sounds people make while in a state of trance or ecstasy.

Felicitas Goodman studied tapes of speaking in tongues from Christian groups across America, from different races and all backgrounds, people who did not know each other and would have had no way to influence each other. When she analyzed the tapes, she found something amazing. Everywhere that people tongue-spoke, they did so in a precise highly regular rhythm—much more regular than ordinary speech or even poetry. And everywhere the rhythm was the same. To

Playing with Sound

If you want to experience something similar to glossolalia, you do not need to go into a full trance. Young children do it spontaneously, and some poets add it to performances of their work. You can experiment with it on its own or in a ritual. Move in a rhythmic way (a slow rhythm works better) before your altar, or as part of a circle, or in a sacred space. Let your breathing become deeper and aligned with the rhythm. Give yourself time to surrender to the movement. When it feels right, simply allow yourself to pour out syllables of sound. Doing it with a small child is both a fun activity and a way to overcome your own self-consciousness. You will find that such wordless chanting liberates a spontaneous creativity.

Goodman this meant that glossolalia was not something people made up, but the outer sign of something very real that happens in the body during trance.

She began to study trance in general. Soon students were asking her to put them into a trance state. Because she happened to be in the American Southwest and had seen a Native American use a gourd rattle, she, too, used that method. She told her students to lie or sit or move about in whatever way helped them focus on the sound. All of them experienced vivid sensations and images. Strangely, these varied tremendously. Goodman was puzzled. If trance was physical, shouldn't the same sound produce roughly the same experiences? She read a research article on meditation. The writer commented that different disciplines called for different postures, and that these postures seemed to influence the meditative response. How obvious, she thought. Our postures influenced our blood flow, heartbeat, and breath. Why shouldn't they affect what we experience in trance?

Worldwide Postures

And then Felicitas Goodman had an inspiration. Rather than try out a series of random postures, why not look at material from trance cultures around the world and see if any special postures presented themselves? As well as photos from tribal ceremonies, she looked at religious imagery. When she found similar postures in different cultures, she studied them carefully so that her students could duplicate them as precisely as possible.

The results thrilled her. Over and over particular postures produced particular responses. With no prior discussion, people who followed the Bear Spirit posture found that their heads opened up from behind to receive a powerful flow of energy into their bodies. Another posture came from a photo of an African diviner who sat with his legs bent beneath him to the right, his left hand out to the side, his right hand close to his left calf. When the students did this posture, they found they would feel themselves spin around (even though they did not actually move), and this whirling would give them a sense that could "find out" or "understand."

She began to suspect that she and her students were rediscovering an ancient wisdom once known by people all over the world.

Over time, Goodman discovered thirty postures, a few of which she describes in detail in *Where the Spirits Ride the Wind*. Some aided journeys to the Spirit world; some had more practical uses, such as divination or healing.

Ritual emerged as an important feature of her work. At the start of one session the image of an old man appeared before her. She acknowledged him as a Spirit who had come to help her, and from then on she would call on her "Friend" to join the session.

Finally, Felicitas Goodman came to understand that the ordinary world and the Spirit world are two halves of a whole. Just as our lives are incomplete without a connection to the Spirits, so they, too, can fulfill themselves only through a connection to physical bodies. The trance journeys, in their different postures, allow these encounters to happen.

Spiral Dancing

Just as Felicitas Goodman discovered postures as entrances to the Spirit world, so Starhawk describes Wiccan rituals as ways to reawaken powers in the human mind. Both posture and movement figure very strongly in this reawakening. When the Witch stands with feet firmly planted on the ground and the athame pointed at the sky in her outstretched arm, she (or he) can feel power course through her and into the Earth. I sometimes have done this posture apart from any particular ritual, as a way to open my body to sacred energy.

The title of Starhawk's most famous book, *The Spiral Dance*, comes from the energy generated in ritual movement. The universe, Starhawk says, is not a collection of separate objects but a continuous energy pattern, always fluid, unstoppable. Energy moves in spirals, cyclic but never returning to the same exact pattern. Spirals are everywhere in nature. Our lives, too, spiral. We cannot stay always in one mode but need to follow our own shifts of energy. And we never return exactly to a previous state.

Begin in a circle with everyone facing in. The one to lead the dance drops the hand of the person on her left and begins to move toward the center in a clockwise (deosil) pattern. Holding hands, the others follow her. When she reaches the center, she turns about to the left to face the person following her. She keeps moving. Since everyone else will have to turn, everybody eventually passes everyone else.

When the leader finds herself outside the spiral, facing out, she should continue about a quarter of the way around, then turn again to face the person following her. As everyone turns they will find them-selves outside the spiral, facing in. When the leader

Starhawk's spiral dance

comes to a loop, where she previously had turned, she goes inside the loop (under-neath the arms of two of the dancers), and once more heads back to the center. Now the group has gone clockwise (inward), counterclockwise (outward), and once more turned clockwise. As the leader winds the spiral tighter and tighter toward the cen-ter, the group chants, wordlessly, so that the pure sound will intensify the power. It all sounds complicated, but in practice it goes smoothly. You and your group might want to rehearse the movements before the actual ritual.

Postures of Surrender

Felicitas Goodman writes of the use of postures in deep trance work. There is a kind of posture that is much more accessible, and yet, in its own way, at least as powerful. These are the bows, prostrations, and hands together in prayer that we find over and over in the world's ritual traditions.

Bowing and other postures help us go beyond our ego's insistence on our own power and independence. They are gestures of surrender. When we seek our own meaningful relation to divine truth, however we conceive it, a bow or prostration becomes an act that brings both joy and peace. It joins us to power rather than takes power away from us. The same Shaker hymn we cited (p. 105), "Simple Gifts," reminds us that "when true simplicity is gained / To bow and to bend / We shan't be ashamed."

Try this experiment. Go to a place where you feel safe and comfortable. If you have an altar, go there and face it, though you do not really need an outward manifestation. You also could try this in some special place in nature. Stand still and take a few deep breaths. Feel the way the floor or the ground supports you. Feel the strength of the Earth below and the vastness of the sky above. Continue to breathe deeply until you desire to express your sense of peace. Place your palms together with the sides of the thumbs against your upper chest so that you can incline your head and touch your lips to the tips of your fingers. Breathe into this posture. Feel your chest rise and fall against your hands. If you wish to visualize a sacred image or say a silent prayer, do so. They are not necessary. Peace lies in the posture itself.

Such movements give us a wonderful sense of return. They take us away from our hectic schedules. They restore us, for a moment, to our true selves.

We have completed our look at the senses and how we use them in ritual. In so doing we discovered how we express ourselves through our bodies. In the next two chapters we will look at the way we create rituals from two main aspects of the world around us—space and time.

𝒟   RESOURCES   𝒟

BOOKS

Deren, Maya. *Divine Horsemen: The Living Gods of Haiti.* Kingston, N.Y.: McPherson & Co., 1985.

Goodman, Felicitas. *Where the Spirits Ride the Wind.* Bloomington, Ind.: Indiana University Press, 1990.

Khan, Pir Vilayat. *The Call of the Dervish, Reprint Edition.* New Lebanon, N.Y.: Omega Press, 1992.

Natale, Frank, *Trance Dance: The Dance of Life.* Rockport, Mass.: Element Books, 1995.

Roth, Gabrielle, *Sweat Your Prayers.* New York: Putnam, 1997.

Skees, Suzanne. *God Among the Shakers.* New York: Hyperion, 1998.

Starhawk. *The Spiral Dance, 10th Anniversary Edition.* San Francisco: HarperSanFrancisco, 1989.

VIDEOS AND CDS

Dancing: Lord of the Dance. Home Vision (800–262–8600). Program two of an eight-part series on all aspects of dance, this video contains footage of ritual dance in India, Africa, and the West with commentary on the history of sacred dance.

Mesko, Sabrina. *Mudra, Gestures of Power.* Sounds True Video.

Roth, Gabrielle. *Endless Wave: Volume One.* Raven (P.O. Box 2034, Red Bank, NJ 07701). Just one of Roth's many CDs designed for ecstatic dance.

Smith, Huston. *Islamic Mysticism: The Sufi Way.* Available from Explorations (800–720–2114). Video containing footage of whirling dervishes.

Three

❖

Ritual in Time and Space

7.

Sacred Time

You rush about in your daily life from one errand to another, filling your desk or refrigerator with to-do lists that never quite get done. But tonight will be different, for this is the night of the Full Moon, and your group has planned a special ritual. You dress in your best clothes, with your silver Moon amulet around your neck. You arrive at your friend's house on the edge of a woods and stand outside with the others, trading stories of your hectic lives. Inside, a bell sounds and a thrill goes through you. With that piercing note the world changes. Silently you enter the room. In the center a circle of flower petals surrounds a circle of rock salt enclosing a single large candle in a silver holder. You feel like you have entered another time, another life.

The World of Ritual

Ritual takes us into another world, a mysterious place of wonder we call "the sacred." For whatever the length of the ritual, be it a few moments in the morning or a weeklong retreat, we step outside our ordinary lives into heightened awareness. Certain moments in life seem to call for the recognition of a ceremony. Rabbi Arthur Waskow, who combines traditional Judaism with environmental activism, describes ritual as the crystallization of our relationship to the world. That relationship is one of rhythms. With our electric lights, and our cars and televisions, and our heated and air-conditioned homes, we forget that we still are creatures of night and day, Summer and Winter, light and dark, New Moon and Full.

In this chapter, we will rediscover the importance of natural time and how we celebrate time in ritual. We will discover how cycles of the Sun and Moon affect us. We will look at ways to mark the seasons. We will develop a personal connection to the Moon with its many phases. And finally we will see how ritual can renew one of the oldest customs in our society, the Sabbath.

Sun and Moon

Most time-oriented rituals are based on the movements of the Sun and Moon. Traditionally, solar rituals are big and grand, based on the Earth's vast annual orbit of the Sun. The opportunities for lunar rituals are more frequent, for we can do them every month if we wish, and not just one ritual but as many as four, for the waxing, the full, the waning, and the new. And yet the lunar rituals are no less powerful.

We will look first at rituals of the Sun.

The Pendulum of the Sun

In the Earth's temperate zones, where most of us live, the seasons are a major part of our lives. Even with all our technologies, we still experience the harshness of Winter, the joy of Spring, the melancholy beauty of Autumn, the swelter and freedom of Summer. The changes in climate come with changes of light that affect us far more than we usually acknowledge. It is not just a question of being optimistic as the light increases in Spring, or depressed in Winter. The changing length of the day is the very rhythm of our universal Mother, the Earth, in her dance with the Sun.

There are four special days that especially mark this relationship: the Summer Solstice, the longest day of the year, when the Sun rises and sets on the northernmost points of the eastern and western horizon lines; the Winter Solstice, the shortest day, when the Sun rises and sets on the southernmost points of the horizon; and the two Equinoxes, when the Sun rises due east and sets due west.

Think of the Sun as a huge pendulum. It swings from one Solstice to the other, and at the exact halfway point in each direction, when it seems to poise for a moment, is an Equinox. The Solstices teach us about Extremes, the Equinoxes about balance. Together, the four days remind us that Earth and sky are one and that all our lives take part in the cycles of the cosmos.

Each of the days has its own character. The Spring Equinox is a day of celebration and hope as the year moves from a time of darkness to one of light. The Summer Solstice, the end of the pendulum, contains sadness within its outer pleasures, for the year begins to move the other way. The ancient Chinese referred to this day as The Wounding of the Bright, and saw in it a lesson that if you push a good situation too far it will reach its limit and eventually slide into its opposite. We experience this truth in many areas of our lives.

The Autumn Equinox is characterized by introspection. This is the time of the harvest and the dying light as the year winds down to the shortest day. The Winter Solstice is the opposite of Summer, a time to celebrate the rebirth of the light from deepest darkness. Of the four days, the Winter Solstice is the most frequently celebrated, simply because it signals hope to witness such a profound change. Christmas, the Pagan Yule, Chanukah, New Year's, and many other holidays from around the world all celebrate the fact that once more the days have begun to lengthen. In a great many of these traditions, people give gifts, especially to children.

Monuments to Light

Stonehenge, in England. Newgrange, in Ireland. Chichen Itza, in Mexico. The Temple of Karnak, in Egypt. All of these monuments, as well as others, such as markings high on canyon walls in the United States, have one thing in common. They all mark the Solstices or Equinoxes. Ancient people saw these days as so significant that they have built entire artificial hills, or moved thirty-five-ton stones into giant circles, in order to celebrate them.

In chapter 3 we described the wonder of the Winter sunrise penetrating the cavelike passage of Newgrange. In fact, the pre-Celtic peoples who built this miracle of engineering did not stop there. A few miles away are two more artificial hills, today called Knowth and Dowth. Knowth, which is even larger than Newgrange, contains two passages, one opening due east, for the Equinox sunrises, and the other due west, for the Equinox sunsets. Dowth has not been restored. It looks like a tree-covered hill with a small cave at the base, until you look closely and see the beautiful engravings on the stones that form the "hill's" foundation. Dowth's passage is aligned to the Winter Solstice sun*set*, the opposite of Newgrange's.

Let us imagine a special yearlong ritual performed through the seasons in Stone Age Ireland. Perhaps it occurred every seven years. It would begin at Newgrange on the morning of the Winter Solstice. The next event would take place at sunrise of the Spring Equinox, celebrated in the eastern passage of Knowth. We do not know of any passage mounds for the Summer Solstice, so perhaps this was celebrated in the open in some way. Then, in the Autumn Equinox, it would return to Knowth, this time to the western passage, for the sunset. Finally, it would end in the chamber of Dowth, at sunset on the Winter Solstice. Imagine the effect of seeing an entire year as a cycle of rituals. At every moment through the struggles of your daily life, you would know that you were part of a yearlong ceremony.

Your Own Solar Rituals

Luckily, you do not have to just imagine solar rituals. You can do them. There are many ways to celebrate the Solstices and Equinoxes, either alone or in groups.

There are general ways to mark the seasons. One thing you can do is go to a sacred place. As we will see in the next chapter, planning a journey to a recognized site can be a wonderful thing to do for your vacation, but you don't have to travel far. There are many more places to mark the Solstices and Equinoxes than we would expect. A little research may turn out some sights close to home. For years, a group met regularly in upstate New York to travel to small structures aligned to Solstice or Equinox sunrises in the Hudson Valley. New Hampshire contains Mystery Hill, a circle of wooden columns described as "the American Stonehenge." The American Southwest has Chaco Canyon. Illinois has Monk's Mound, the

Personal Rituals at Solar Sites

If you do find a local site—say, a stone structure aligned to the Winter Solstice—and it's on private property, make sure you get permission beforehand. Tell the owner what you want to do and that you will not disturb anything. You will need something to set out in honor of the light—a small crystal works well—some food, such as a piece of fruit, and incense. Stand inside the structure (or circle) and place the crystal at the entrance. Before the actual sunrise, burn the incense to honor the ancestors who have created the site and done rituals before you. As the smoke rises, feel it join you to the past.

As the sky lightens, watch the light, breathe into it, let it carry you into a light trance. Let your imagination carry you back in time. See what spontaneous images come up of ancient celebrations. You may surprise yourself with the vividness of your images.

When the sky is fully light, eat the fruit. Leave a small piece for the birds or animals. Before you leave, make sure you pack up whatever you brought.

largest earth structure in the world, two and a half times the size of the Great Pyramid in Egypt. All these places, and many more, mark the seasons.

If you are lucky enough to live near the Atlantic or Pacific Ocean, you have a natural way to celebrate the Equinoxes. There are few sights more exciting than seeing the Sun rise out of the Atlantic or set in the Pacific. Bring a small offering, such as cornmeal, to cast to the wind. A rattle can help you breathe into the vision of the Sun's glory. You won't need much else. The Sun will inspire you. Sing to it. Open your arms to it. Dance if you feel like it. You may wish to end your ritual with a bow and a blessing of gratitude. (WARNING: Never look directly at the Sun. You can damage your eyes. You do not need to stare at it to experience its wonder.)

A special opportunity comes when there is a Full Moon on the Equinox, for then the Moon rises in the east at the same time the Sun sets in the west. Once, I went to a women's retreat just before the Autumn Equinox. On the last day of the retreat, I led a ritual of connection to ancient roots and then headed home. As sunset neared, I remembered it was the day after the Equinox and the anniversary

Creating Your Own Solar Site

You also can create a solar site at your own home or on the roof of your apartment building. The Equinoxes are simpler, since you just have to align your stones, or whatever you choose to set out, along an east-west axis. To find the line of the Solstices is not that much harder. Your local librarian could help you research the information. If you have the opportunity to make a permanent circle on your own property, gather stones you find especially striking. Mark out the axis you want in the dirt and then lay some of the stones in a double line along that axis. This creates a symbolic avenue for the light. At the end of the double line place a large stone or a statue of a mythological figure you associate with the Sun. Make that the center of the circle. The avenue will then be the circle's radius, and you can lay the rest of the stones around the center. You probably will not see the actual sunrise, unless you are lucky enough to build your circle on a high hill. You will, however, have your own sacred marker for solar rituals.

of a special trip I had taken to a sacred site in Greece. I stopped by a small hill and climbed it just as the Sun was setting on one side of the sky and the Moon was rising on the other. With arms outstretched, I breathed in the wonder of the perfect balance of Sun and Moon.

Rituals for the Spring Equinox

The Spring Equinox is a wonderful moment. Winter has ended, the world is returning to life. Flowers are budding or in bloom, and from now on the days will get longer and brighter.

People all over the world have developed elaborate rituals to bring out the special qualities of Spring. What follows is one modern example, modified from Starhawk's book *The Spiral Dance*. To prepare, place symbols in each of the four cardinal directions. In the East, the direction of mind, burn incense. Place a box of

A Tree for the Spring

Something simple, yet with great meaning, that you can do on the Spring Equinox is plant a tree. Do it with ceremony and in honor of the Earth and the Sun. Say a prayer as you plant it. Make the tree an offering of hope, and speak of what you want to see grow in your own life. As it takes root and grows, you will see your own visions grow with it. You can make the tree an offering of healing for a sick family member, or in honor of someone who has died. To do this, place a photo or memento of the person at the base of the new tree.

Finish the ritual by placing some simple decoration on it. You can hang a small pendant from one of the stronger branches, or put a beautiful stone at the base. At later rituals, especially for future Equinoxes or Solstices, decorate the tree further. This will make it an ongoing creation. If you have dedicated it to a dead relative, the tree will bring his or her presence into any rituals you do there.

dirt in the North, for the body. A bowl of water symbolizes emotions in the West; a fire in the South represents Spirit (make sure the fire is carefully contained). As everyone stands in the circle, one person who has taken the role of priest goes around with black wool. He asks each person, "What binds you?" Someone might answer, "Fear of the unknown." He wraps the person's wrists and repeats the person's own words: "Fear of the unknown binds you."

After the priest has bound the people, the person serving as priestess asks each one, "Where must you go to be free?" They each say the direction that suits the quality they need. If they need clarity of thought, they will say, "The East." If they need physical healing, they will say, "The North." Then each person goes to the place and passes their bonds over or through the earth, fire, and so on. Now the group begins a wordless chant. When it reaches its peak, the priestess shouts, "Now!" Everyone pulls apart their bonds and dances or sings or shouts. When the energy dies down, the circle re-forms for quiet meditation, after which the priestess gathers flowers in her arms and offers them to each person, saying, "Take what you need." They each take a flower whose color inspires them. End the ritual with a feast.

Summer Solstice

The Summer Solstice is a celebration of light and warmth even as the Sun begins to diminish. Many mythologies associate the Sun with a god who is born at the Winter Solstice, grows through the Spring, is sacrificed at his peak on the Summer Solstice, then travels through the underworld in the growing darkness of the Autumn Equinox to be reborn once more at the next Winter Solstice. One way to celebrate this cycle is to create an effigy of some kind—woven of straw or sticks, carved, whatever will burn—to sacrifice in a fire at the end of the long day of light.

The shift from light to dark should not dim the celebration of Summer. Many people cover an altar with flowers, or make flower wreaths that they wear on their heads. The day is a time for dancing and feasting. If you celebrate alone or with family, it is a perfect day to make a tree shrine (see chapter 3). The shrine will honor the light and create something to last through the coming darkness. If you celebrate with a group, it is a wonderful day for a procession with flowers, and colorful banners, and statues or pictures of gods and goddesses of the Sun. You do not need to adopt any belief system to enjoy such images. The procession can begin at a meeting place and move to the ritual site, which should be prepared beforehand with such things as food tables and an unlit fire. The day is also a good time to tell stories of Sun gods and goddesses. You can gather in a circle at a quiet time in the day and share tales from mythology. Make these as vivid as possible. As the Sun sinks, light the fire.

Autumn Equinox and Winter Solstice

The Autumn Equinox is a time of harvest, but also of introspection. The day and night are in balance, but we know the year is moving toward the dark and cold of Winter. While some people honor the Equinox in groups, with a more spiritual version of Thanksgiving, others prefer to spend it alone, perhaps going to a special place in nature. Instead of doing an elaborate ritual, they walk among the falling leaves. However you choose to celebrate it, the Autumn Equinox is a good time to reflect on what you have "harvested" in your life in the past year.

The Winter Solstice is the celebration of rebirth. Even though we call it the beginning rather than the end of Winter, and in northern climates months of cold and snow remain, the days now get longer. Light is returning to the world. To signify hope in the midst of cold, people often give gifts at this time of year. The following ritual uses gift giving in a spiritual way.

The ritual takes place in evening. Arrange cushions and chairs in a circle. Set a small candle to burn in the center, with unlit candles, in protected holders, before each cushion or chair. Set up the ritual area beforehand and then cover all the food tables and decorations with black crepe paper. All the people wear something dark and shroudlike over their clothes. Each person also carries some object that symbolizes something significant in her or his life from the past year.

The people enter one by one and silently set their objects in the center around the lit candle, then take a spot on a cushion or chair. When everyone is seated, people breathe deeply together until there is a feeling of having settled into the ritual. Then someone allows intuition to guide them to an object in the center. He or she speaks briefly about what made him or her choose it, and then the person who brought it tells its story. Now that person chooses an object, until finally everyone has received someone else's symbol and told her or his story.

Everyone sits in silence and then someone begins a hum or wordless chant. When the energy has built to a peak, the person who first chose cries, "Rejoice in the birth of light!" With a wordless shout, everyone lights their candles. As light fills the room, people fling off their dark coverings (be careful of the candles!) to reveal white or brightly colored clothes underneath. Quickly people remove the crepe paper from the tables to reveal food and cheerful decorations. The rest of the evening is spent in celebration until the circle rejoins to end the ritual. Everyone takes home the object she or he chose from the giveaway.

The Cross-Quarter Days

The Ancient Celts of Western Europe saw the year as a great Wheel with eight rather than four significant points. Along with the Solstices and Equinoxes they celebrated the Cross-Quarter Days, the moments halfway between the solar events. To do this gives your year a fuller sense of ritual movement, for you are never more than forty-five days from a major day of ceremony.

This Celtic calendar of holidays is more than a historical curiosity. The modern Wiccan religion has adopted it and modified it for contemporary truths. While they have kept most of the Celtic traditions, they also have blended in other deities. The Witches call these eight days "Sabbats."

Some of these days are known to modern culture under secular guises. For example, Groundhog Day, February 2, actually comes from the celebration of the first stirrings of Spring, known to the Celts as *Imbolc*, Candlemas, and Bridget's Day. Bridget (called Bridey in Scotland) was the Irish goddess of fire. When the Irish converted to Christianity they renamed the goddess St. Bridget, and her day of celebration remained.

Between the Spring Equinox and the Winter Solstice comes Beltane, the first of May, a time of great joy. After the Summer Solstice the mood of the year shifts toward Autumn and the fading light. *Lughnasad*, on August 1, celebrates the early harvest.

The final Cross-Quarter Day, October 31, was originally called *Samhain*, the Celtic New Year. Later it became known as All Hallows' Eve, and then Halloween.

The Wiccan May Day

Of all the Witches' Sabbats, Beltane, the first of May, is possibly the most joyous, with its famous dance around the Maypole.

1. Set up the Maypole and hang it with flowers and multicolored ribbons. Fill bushes and tree branches with fruits, more flowers, and cookies and doughnuts.

2. Build a fire in the south of the celebration ground.

3. Each person chooses a ribbon from the pole. They say the color aloud and its meaning: "I choose red, for passion," or "I choose green, for new life."

4. As people on the side play or sing, the dancers weave the ribbons in and out of each other. They visualize weaving their desire into their lives.

5. When the ribbons have wound tightly around the pole, the celebrants release them and continue dancing.

6. Now they begin to leap over the bonfire, an act of purification, and call out the thing they desire to see grow in the Summer warmth. Lovers jump together.

7. The ritual ends as the celebrants feast on the fruit and cakes hanging on the trees and bushes.

Originally, it was the Celtic New Year. Now it has become the New Year of the Witches. Like the Celts, the Wiccans believe that the moment between the old year and the new is a very special time, when the "Veil Between the Worlds" stretches thin. Spirits can enter the world, and the living can commune with the dead. The Celts considered it a dangerous time (the source of all those spooky Halloween stories), but also a time of opportunity, for on Samhain we are most able to see into the future, either through direct trance communication or through some system of divination. For many people, reading Tarot cards on Samhain is a must.

The use of these Cross-Quarter Days is not just a way to fill in the festival year. They actually mark changes in the Earth. Fara Shaw Kelsey, a Hudson Valley herbalist and healer to whom many people turn for knowledge of the rhythms of nature, teaches that despite the deep cold of February, Spring really does begin around February 2. Look closely and you will see buds begin to form on the trees. And in August, when it seems like it can't get any hotter, look at the tops of trees and you will see that the first leaves have begun to turn color.

The Power of the Moon

The light of the Moon is softer, more mysterious, and more subtle than the Sun's. And yet it can stir us on a very deep level. There are even direct physical effects.

According to Zsuzsanna E. Budapest (often called simply Z), author of *Grandmother Moon*, baby deliveries increase dramatically twenty-four hours before a Full Moon. Under a waxing Moon, our skin breaks out more easily and we bleed

Moon phases

more in surgery. Cut your hair during a waxing Moon phase and it will grow more quickly. When the Moon wanes, we heal more quickly from surgery. For many people the waning Moon is a good time to finish things, a bad time to start projects, and a terrible time to sign a contract. Z. Budapest suggests that if you need a new home you should search for it under a New Moon, move while the Moon waxes, and try to clean it up and get settled while the Moon wanes.

And the Full Moon? In *Grandmother Moon* Z says, "The Full Moon is good only for ritual, lovemaking, and dancing."

People who resist the lunar rhythms and try to treat every day as the same sometimes experience strong emotions during the Full Moon. The word "lunacy" comes from the Latin word *Luna,* for Moon. The legend of werewolves says that men become wolves under the light of the Full Moon. Such stories are fantastic metaphors for the wild quality the Moon stirs in us. Yet if we accept the Moon's subtleties and changing shapes and light, it can become our greatest ally in understanding our own moods and emotions.

Talking to the Moon

In many areas of ritual we make the forces of nature more real by speaking to them. Z Budapest describes a ceremony in which she talked with "Grandmother Moon." Speaking silently, she asked, "What is the most important thing we can learn from you?"

The answer formed in her mind: "To flow. Don't be afraid to let go. Don't be afraid to become full. Don't be afraid."

We can talk to the Moon and feel her energy so strongly in ritual because she is a real presence in the sky that constantly changes. The Moon is born each month out of darkness, grows, becomes full and luminous (with that marvelous appearance of a face that looks down at us with such gentleness and peace), then diminishes, smaller and smaller, until once more the dark night swallows it. Thus the Moon, even more than the Sun, is a model of death and rebirth. It teaches us, in fact, that we go through this process many times in our lives. Every month the Moon gives us the chance to experience our own life, death, and rebirth. Moon rituals allow us to consciously connect ourselves with the lunar phases.

Special Lunar Rituals

Lunar rituals can also be annual events. One very special lunar holiday is the Chinese New Year, which falls each year between January 15 and February 15. In San Francisco there are parades, with bands and athletic contests, and fireworks to honor the gods, and firecrackers to scare off evil Spirits.

You do not need to live near a Chinatown to celebrate this wonderful holiday. Many calendars or newspapers will give the details. Light white candles and sprinkle salt on them so the flame crackles to feed the Spirits. Set off firecrackers and sparklers. Give a feast in honor of the ancestors, and serve oranges for good fortune and a whole fish for prosperity. Fill your altar and the table with flowers and fresh fruit. Near my home in upstate New York, outside a tiny community in the mountains, there is a Chinese Buddhist temple with five separate buildings, each with its own statues of the Buddha (one building has five hundred gold painted Buddhas, each in a different posture). When I went there for New Year's with a friend who was raised in Hong Kong, we found all the altars filled with wonderful flowers and fruit and incense.

Remember—when you celebrate Chinese New Year, make sure you spread molasses on the lips of the kitchen god!

Chinese New Year rituals do not stop with the New Moon. On the three days of the Full Moon in the first month after the New Year lanterns are hung everywhere, on doors, porches, outside homes, on the graves of ancestors. There are fireworks, and fairs for artisans. A special figure of this time is the Moon goddess Chang-Mu. She was once a mortal woman, married to an archer. When the gods sought to reward her husband with the elixir of immortality, Chang-Mu drank it down herself. Immortal now, she fled to the Moon, where the Hare of the Moon protected her.

A Daily Ritual

The Sun and Moon provide a great framework for rituals of life's rhythms. However, you do not need to wait for special times of the year, or phases of the Moon, to perform rituals. In some religious traditions, people perform rituals

Daily Blessings

Here is an experiment you can try. For a week, each morning when you wake up, before you worry about what to wear or the endless to-do lists, go to your altar. If you do not have an altar, choose a special object that for you symbolizes spirituality and set it somewhere no one will disturb it.

Take a few deep breaths. Breathe gently and allow the air to go all the way down on the in breath, all the way released on the out. Feel how the oxygen wakes up your body. Be aware of your feet on the floor, of your posture. Be aware of the day, if it's sunny or cloudy, be aware of any noise or movement (you should tell your family ahead of time that you need this moment for yourself). Recognize that disturbances exist, but they exist outside you.

Focus now on the object you have set out. See it as an opening to sacred energy. Continue to breathe deeply and realize that you, too, your body and your life, open to the sacred. Say a short prayer or blessing. You can say it silently or aloud, whichever feels right. It can be as simple as "I thank you, God, for the wonder and beauty of this moment."

End with a "seal," such as the Jewish/Christian "Amen," or the Wiccan "Blessed be." Place your palms together and bow your head once. Spend another moment or two in that realm of peace, then take a step backward. You are now ready to begin the day.

Try this for a week. If you feel foolish or critical, just accept that. See if it changes. After a week you may find that you wish to abandon the practice and go back to your normal routine. You also may decide to go a little further, with slightly longer blessings, incense, or some act of divination, like choosing a Tarot card for the day. Remember, an experiment is just that—a way to see what works for you.

every day. Jews bless their food, say a prayer upon waking and before sleep, when they wash themselves, or when they make love. Devout Catholics may say their rosary every day, as do Buddhists. Muslims pray five times a day toward Mecca. All this may seem very tedious—do we really want to stop and say a prayer before we make love? Suppose you did it because you wanted to do it, because it connected you to an energy and a beauty beyond the hectic pace of daily life?

A Day of Rest

Did your family celebrate the Sabbath when you were growing up? Did your parents wake you early on Sunday to go to church and Sunday school? And did you then go home, or maybe to Grandma's house, for Sunday dinner? If you grew up with this pattern, you may have mixed feelings about the idea of a day of rest. It may surprise you, then, that thousands of Christians and Jews have begun to look forward each week to the Sabbath, not as a time of obligations or rules, but as a genuine renewal.

Rabbi David Cooper, author of *Renewing Your Soul: A Guided Retreat for the Sabbath and Other Days of Rest*, teaches the Sabbath as a chance to step back and become aware of your own spirituality. While he follows the Jewish pattern, he emphasizes a mindfulness similar to Zen. You do not need to be Jewish, or Christian, to make use of a one-day retreat. In the descriptions that follow, I have adapted the traditions to general spiritual practice.

For a full Sabbath retreat, preparation is vital. You need to buy whatever you will need so you do not have to break the rhythm by a dash to the Kwik-E-Mart. Try to clean the house, so the environment feels renewed, and cook your food ahead of time so it will be there when you need it.

Try to release anger or clear up tensions so you can give your full attention to the joys of spiritual rest. Clearly, this will not always be possible. The candle-lighting ceremony gives you a chance to step back from any leftover problems. As a final preparation, tell friends and co-workers that you will not be available for twenty-four hours. Turn off the ringer on your telephones and the volume on your answering machine. This is your time to look inward.

Candle Lighting

The Jewish Sabbath begins at sundown with candles. For many Jewish women their favorite religious memory is of their mothers lighting candles on Friday nights.

Use two candlesticks and candles that can burn safely all the way down. Before the lighting, spend five or ten minutes allowing yourself to settle into a meditative state. Reflect on the past week and all that has happened. Whether good or bad, tell yourself that you can let go of it for the next day.

Look outside for a moment. Watch the light change color, fade in the sky. When you strike the match, watch the flash of light, see how it brings the candles to life.

After you light the candles sweep your arms three times above them, as if to gather the light into your heart and soul. Close your eyes for a moment and say a blessing. Express your gratitude for this perfect moment, this oasis of rest.

After the candle ceremony, spend another five or ten minutes in contemplation. Think about yourself and your family and friends. This is a time to ask for what you need. You might ask for healing for a sick friend, or renewed love in an estranged relationship, or success in your job search. If you ask with the ritual awareness of the sacred, you will find that the things you seek are beyond selfishness.

The next day, continue your spiritual rest. Do not drive (especially not to the mall!). Go for walks, watch the world around you, read instead of watching television. As evening approaches, reflect on the experience of rest and any insights that may have come to you.

To end your retreat, go outside for a moment (if you live in an apartment building, you may want to go up on the roof). Raise your arms to the sky, then touch the Earth or floor. Call on the divine energy to support you and those you love in the coming week.

Time is one aspect of our physical existence. We also walk on the physical Earth. For as long as humanity has existed, people have recognized certain places as special. In the next chapter, we will look at how we can identify sacred places and use them in our own rituals.

✐   RESOURCES   ✐

BOOKS

Budapest, Zsuzanna E. *Grandmother Moon.* San Francisco: HarperSanFrancisco, 1991.

Cooper, David A. *Renewing Your Soul: A Guided Retreat for the Sabbath and Other Days of Rest.* San Francisco: HarperSanFrancisco, 1995.

Heinberg, Richard. *Celebrating the Solstice.* Wheaton, Ill.: Quest Books, 1993.

Rechtschaffen, Stephan. *Timeshifting: Creating More Time to Enjoy Your Life.* New York: Doubleday, 1977.

Reid, Lori. *Moon Magic: How to Use the Moon's Phases to Inspire and Influence Your Relationships, Home Life and Business.* New York: Three Rivers Press, 1998.

WEB SITES

Z Budapest lists a month-by-month calendar of ancient holidays on her site, www.netwizards.net/Zbudapest.

To get in tune with the larger cycles of time as reflected in the planets and stars, many resources for amateur astronomers are available at www.astronomy.com.

8.

Sacred Space

Slowly, without hurry, you climb the hill, the path that winds back and forth like an ancient serpent embedded in the Earth. Only when you get to the top do you see the great rock mound, thousands of years old. Myth tells how the mound holds the sleeping body of the Queen of the Otherworld. You climb to the top and stare out at the sea. The beach is below you, with two curved peninsulas that reach out into the water like welcoming arms for the sailors who would have found shelter in the protected bay. Behind you, the shimmering lake curves around as if to form a circle with the salt water. And beyond the lake, the mountains rear up, protecting the entire landscape. Now you close your eyes. You can sense the energy surge up through the deep places in the Earth, feel the way the mound shapes and holds it and releases it through the surrounding land. When you open your eyes, two gulls circle each other in the sky above you.

The Power of Sacred Places

The site described above is Maeve's Cairn, on top of the hill of Knocknarea, on the west coast of Ireland. An earth mound covered with stones, it has stood for thousands of years overlooking the bay. No one has ever excavated the cairn. The local people have always refused permission, for they believe it to be the burial site of Queen Maeve, described both as a warrior queen from the early Celts, and the queen of the *Sidhe*, or Faerie people. The cairn is said to be hollow, an actual entrance to the world of the Spirits.

Knocknarea is only one of thousands of sites, places where ancient peoples have observed some special quality of the landscape or the energy of the Earth itself, and marked it with a monument. Today, more and more people are traveling to these places as well as discovering similar wonders closer to home.

Such sites, as impressive as they are, are only one kind of sacred place. There are also the churches, temples, and mosques. There are sacred groves of trees, and caves and grottoes painted with pictures as old as fifty thousand years. There are also the sacred places we make ourselves.

We have seen how the different senses—sight and sound, taste, smell, and touch—contribute to the power of rituals, and we have seen how strong it can be to align our ritual practice with time. Physical places, both natural and constructed, can also contribute to the wonder of ritual experience. The space that we inhabit and move through is an essential part of any ritual. Sometimes we create that space ourselves, through the ways we use a room, the altars we set up, the fires we light, the circles we cast, the dances and chants we perform. There are also recognized ritual places of many kinds, each with its own energy, its own special lesson.

Common Traits of Sacred Places

Sacred sites, especially the older ones, often have certain things in common. For one thing, they are places of natural beauty. We have seen how ritual needs to engage the senses for maximum effect. A peaceful setting is also important, for it allows people who come there to step back from ordinary life in order to experience the special qualities of sacred ritual.

Older sites often have more subtle qualities. In modern society, people build a church wherever the building committee can manage to buy an attractive property. Many of the old churches and cathedrals of Europe, however, were built over Pagan ritual sites. And the Pagan structures stood over older Stone Age places that were not chosen at random but were places where underground springs burst up onto the surface. The springs carried energy and also symbolized the lifeblood of the Earth goddess. Some places were seen as especially powerful because the water that burst out of the rock was hot, or filled with iron that turned it red, the color of blood.

Many sacred places also carry electromagnetic energy. This is something that dowsers, people who use a wooden rod to detect water and other energy, have known for years. Now sensitive instruments have begun to measure the power that wells up in these places of underground streams. Marty Cain, who teaches the creation of sacred space, has studied such sites for years. She describes how the water pushing up to the surface forms a spiral of energy that lifts up into the sky. This draws down a similar spiral of energy from above. The two together form a double helix, the same shape as the intertwined strands of DNA that form the basis of every living organism.

The symbolic meaning of the place, the image of the Earth's lifeblood, is not a completely separate issue from the electric energy found there. To put such things in separate boxes is a modern habit. Ancient people understood these things as a totality. The water, and the forms of the landscape, and the trees that grew there, and the animals that hovered around, and the caves that opened into the Earth, these all formed the divine body. And that body is alive, something the shamans and other sensitives could feel without the aid of instruments.

When we build a shrine or temple over such a place we do not simply acknowledge it, or make use of it. Instead, we help it emerge into reality. The shape of the structure, the symbolic images, and yes, the rituals that we do there, all of these help bring that divine body into physical reality.

All of this may sound very fanciful, or even worse, abstract. It is not. Once you have experienced it, as I did at Knocknarea, you know just how real it is.

Kinds of Sacred Sites

Churches are the sacred spaces most of us know best. They are meant as places to help people direct their worship. Symbols, such as the Cross, and holy imagery, like the stained glass in the windows, encourage people's awareness. Ideally, churches are places the divine itself comes to inhabit so that when people enter them they know that they stand in the presence of God. Today many people think of churches in a more symbolic way, but others still think of them as God's house.

Churches also benefit from the centuries of tradition behind them. When you enter a church, you understand that this is a space dedicated to worship. If you go to an empty church, or especially a cathedral, you can almost hear the hymns and the priest celebrating mass. Catholic churches often have rows of candles at the back. For a small contribution you can light one and say a prayer. Whatever your own religious background, this is a simple ritual that allows you to touch the energy of an ancient tradition. Similarly, if you are fortunate enough to live near a Buddhist temple, you will find sticks of incense to light as you say a short prayer.

Older sacred sites include the temples of pre-Christian times. Here, too, the grandeur of the buildings, as well as the knowledge we have of what went on there, give us a feeling of the sacred power. The fact that so many of them lie in ruins somehow only adds to the effect. The weathered quality of the rock helps them blend in with nature.

A church

Labyrinths

One very special form of sacred structure is the labyrinth. A labyrinth is not a maze or a puzzle, but a highly formal pattern. Based on spirals, it has the peculiar quality that you enter it about halfway, then move outward, then go in almost to the center, then return to the outermost ring before you finally reach the true center. All of this occurs just by following the path and without crossing any lines. The more rings the labyrinth has, the more the journey moves inward and outward.

Chartres Cathedral labyrinth

You exit a labyrinth the same way you came in. The Rev. Dr. Lauren Artress, canon of Grace Cathedral in San Francisco, and a world expert on labyrinths, suggests that you enter with the knowledge that you will travel to the center of your own truth, and then follow the path back out to return to your outer life.

Though theoretically a labyrinth can have any number of rings, the most common forms have either seven or eleven. Artress describes the seven-ring labyrinth as joyful and extroverted. You feel connected to other people. She sees the eleven-circuit labyrinth as more complex and introspective. Because it takes a longer time to walk, with more turns inward and outward, you become peaceful within yourself. She says that you still feel connected to anyone who is walking it with you, or celebrating a ritual outside the labyrinth, but in a quieter way.

The very act of walking a labyrinth is a ritual. As you move into and out of it, traveling at your own pace, you experience the power of walking a sacred pattern. You know that you will reach the center, and yet you discover that the path—like the path to divine truth—is not a straight line, or even a simple spiral that just gets closer and closer until you are there. Instead, you need to go all the way to the edge in order to reach the innermost point. Many people find this an intense metaphor for their lives.

Your Own Labyrinth

Many people have begun to create their own labyrinths, either on their property, if they have the space, or at a church or spiritual center. Lauren Artress's book *Walking the Labyrinth* gives instructions on how to lay out the pattern. Most people prefer to form the rings out of rocks. You can do this as a group project, with family and friends. Once you have built the form, plant flowers in it, or decorate it with small statues at various points where the pattern turns. Some people build a small mound of rocks in the center. As people walk the labyrinth, they add to the mound. Others prefer to leave the center empty, as a place to meet and ponder what inspiration has come to them on their walk.

Labyrinths invite rituals. Try walking it at night and setting candles at different points on the outside, so that you feel supported by light as you travel your path. If there is a group, everyone chants or hums quietly to support the walkers. The first person who enters waits in the center and gives a crystal to each person as a symbol of illumination. As each of the others leaves, she or he blesses the next person. When the first person, who has waited in the center, finally exits, the entire group joins in a blessing of the paths they have followed, all the same and yet each one different.

Very Old Sites

Prehistoric people marked sacred sites with giant stone structures. These could be as simple as a single upright stone, called a "monolith," or as complex as Stonehenge, the great circle that stands high on a hill in southwestern England. We have already seen (chapter 3) how the stones are arranged so the first rays of the Summer Solstice sunrise fall on a "heelstone" in the center. Modern scientists have correlated a whole range of astronomical events with the arrangement of the stones, so many that "astro-archaeologists" refer to Stonehenge as an observatory. It was even used to mark off a fifty-six-year cycle of eclipses.

There are many stone circles, from England to New Guinea. Some are gigantic. Avebury Circle, not many miles from Stonehenge, is so big an entire village fits in the center of it. You actually can stay in a bed-and-breakfast inside the circle.

Other stone circles are small and intimate. Below Knocknarea, in the fields outside the Irish city of Sligoh, stand a number of circles formed of stones only about three feet high. The farmers who graze their cows in the fields tolerate the occasional visitors who come to stand or sit in their local Stone Age monuments.

An even older way that people have marked sacred spaces is the art found on cave walls and rocks around the world. The great bulls of Lascaux (seventeen thousand years old) are the most famous, but they are not the oldest. Certain rock paintings in Australia have been dated to fifty thousand years ago. The tradition of paintings continues in Australia to this day. Tourists who visit the parts of sacred territory open to outsiders and view the powerful art are sometimes very confused to learn that the "primitive" pictures were done the previous month.

There are also stunning rock paintings in the American Southwest, in such places as Chaco Canyon and Canyon de Chelly. And high on a 430-foot butte in Chaco Canyon, New Mexico, the ancient Anasazi people created an astronomical marker in some ways even more remarkable than Stonehenge. It consists of two spirals carved into stone sheltered by three leaning slabs of rock. At noon each day, light passes through slits between the slabs. At noon on the Summer Solstice, a dagger of light pierces the center of the larger spiral. At the Winter Solstice two daggers of light touch the outsides of that spiral. At the Equinoxes light pierces the center of the smaller spiral. And once every nineteen years a shadow passes through the center of the large spiral, on the day that the Sun rises from a position that will be reached by the Full Moon that same night. The shadow bisects the spiral's rings—nineteen of them—and aligns with a pecked groove. At night the Moon itself casts a shadow tangential to the far left edge of the spiral. What an astonishing wonder this is! Astronomy, surveying, engineering, art perfectly brought together. While the site itself is too inaccessible for rituals on the spot, it must have acted as the signal for rituals below. Today, just to travel to such a place is a ritual.

Ritual Pilgrimages

Taking a journey to a recognized sacred site can be a wondrous experience, the trip of a lifetime.

The sacred sites described earlier are just a fraction of such places around the world. A little research can lead you to a site that has meaning for you. You might find a Native American cairn (small burial mound) just a few miles away. Or you might feel an incredible pull to ancient goddess monuments in Western Turkey. Either way, if you approach the entire journey as a ritual, you may find it the most extraordinary trip you've ever taken.

Let's assume for the moment that you want to go to a very recognized site—say, the temples of ancient Greece. You've read about the gods and goddesses, you've drummed and chanted to the Moon goddesses, you've built an altar to Athena and celebrated the return of Persephone from the Land of the Dead. Now you want to go to the actual places where these stories and rites originated.

Such a trip may seem extravagant, but think of vacations people take at expensive resorts where the only attractions are loud music with an obnoxious DJ, over-

Artemis *Athena* *Aphrodite*

A Serpent in the Earth

In southern Ohio, near the city of Chillicothe, stands one of the world's most magnificent works of art, the Serpent Mound. Built on a ridge of rock that overlooks a narrow, sinuous river, the earthwork sculpture stands about three feet high and forms an undulating serpent a quarter mile long. At the end its mouth opens wide, as if to swallow something. Its creators, whoever they might have been, vanished long ago, leaving it as mysterious as paintings of bulls in French caves.

We do know that serpents have been creatures of sacred power all over the world. Sometimes they signify evil, but in other places they represent wisdom, and especially rebirth, for snakes periodically shed their skins so that they seem to be reborn out of their old selves. This makes the Serpent Mound a perfect place to visit for the Spring Equinox.

If you can go to the Serpent Mound, walk it with a sense of your own transformation. Start at the tail (the park managers have created a path that circles the sculpture). Before you actually walk, close your eyes and think of whatever "dead skin" you want to shed in your life. As you walk toward the head, imagine all these things falling away from you. When you reach the head, stop and think of what things you want to see grow in your life. Continue to think of these things as you return to the tail. When you finish, close your eyes and visualize your new life. Say a blessing of gratitude to the ancestors who created the inspiration for your walk.

You can do this simple ritual with a snake pattern that you yourself lay out on the ground.

rich food and overcomplicated drinks, and a giant swimming pool. Compare that to the Moon on Delphi, where the Sibyls spoke their oracular prophecies thousands of years ago—not to mention stuffed grape leaves and homemade retsina in a local taverna.

Arranged Tours

There are two ways to mount such a trip: either with a tour group or on your own. Currently, there are many group trips to sacred places, usually led by someone who has visited and studied them. Sometimes an archaeologist and spiritual teacher will lead a group together. Some research will uncover tours that include rituals as well as lectures. The advantages to official tours are many. Most obviously, you are following guides who know the material. Second, the tour arranges everything so you do not have to worry about hotels and transportation. Finally, you are going with a group of people with similar goals. Not only may you make some good friends, the rituals you do will gain strength from the group energy.

However, there also are drawbacks. Tours may be expensive, because they tend to use large tourist hotels and restaurants. This not only costs you money, but you also can lose the flavor of the local culture. By contrast, if you take public transportation or rent a small car you cannot help but meet people. And while a tour group can be wonderful for new friends, there is always the danger of one or two people who simply get on everyone's nerves.

Some tour groups try to fill the time with as many sacred sites as possible. When choosing, examine the itinerary carefully. Is there enough time spent at each place? You cannot just look at a sacred site and leave. You need to spend at least a little time to experience it. Luckily, many tours do include free time. While others in your group go for souvenirs or to sample the local restaurants, you can buy some bread and cheese and wine and just sit among the stones, or look at the Earth and sky, or perform your own, more intimate ritual.

Pilgrimages on Your Own

There are great rewards to making your own sacred journey. You can go on your own schedule, stay as long as you like, and change your itinerary whenever you wish. More important, you experience the site in your own way, undirected by any-one else's theories and lectures.

If you do choose to go alone or with a friend, you need to study the places you plan to go ahead of time. Read the history, the mythology, the symbolism, the architecture (if you're going to temples or other structures). Of course, you would want to do this if you went with a group as well. The more prepared you are, the more you will get from the experience.

If you go on a sacred journey by yourself, or with one or two friends, you will have the work, and uncertainty, of finding places to stay near each site you want to visit. Public transport can be rough in some countries, but an adventure all by itself. If you rent a car you face unknown road conditions, especially to reach some of the more remote temples, tombs, or stone circles. In some places, a woman alone has to be careful about where she goes and at what time of day. Usually, if you go with a friend this is not a problem. You may face language problems, though you are more and more likely to find someone in even the smallest towns who speaks at least a little English. If you learn the basics of their language and have a good phrase book, you'll be amazed at how well you can get along.

Preparations and Arrivals

Preparation means more than gathering knowledge. Always remember, this is a rit-ual journey, not a tourist trip. Though you certainly want to enjoy yourself along the way, you also want to allow yourself all the possibilities of a journey of trans-formation.

Preparation begins even before you leave home. You can use ritual as well as information to align yourself to Spirits of the place you want to visit. If you know the deities of the places, find images of them and set them on your altar or around the house. Spend time with them, in meditation or reading their stories. Do ritu-als at home based on their qualities.

If you do not know the specific deities—for instance, if you plan to visit the stone circles—you can create a model of the place, aligned to the same compass

A Ritual for Aphrodite

Suppose you plan to visit temples dedicated to Greek Aphrodite, the goddess of love, whose Roman name is Venus. You can do a ritual to her at home before you set off on your trip.

Choose an evening when the weather report promises clear skies through the night and early morning. Preferably it should be an evening when Venus is bright in the sky. Clean the bedroom as if for a special occasion. Prepare an altar with images of the goddess, plus pictures and scenes that invoke love. You can cut out pictures from magazines. Between two candlesticks put out a vase of fresh red roses, Aphrodite's sacred flower, and seashells, for Aphrodite was born out of the sea at dawn. Finally, include mementos from your own life as well, such as a prom picture or old love letters.

Before you go to sleep, step outside and look at the sky. If you can locate Venus (the brightest object in the sky after the Moon), ask it to send down its light of love and healing to you.

Instead of reading or watching TV before you sleep, pick up some of the mementos from your altar. Let memories, both good and bad, come back to you. If necessary, allow yourself to cry.

Set your alarm so you can bathe yourself at first light, then dress and adorn yourself at sunrise. Wear gold jewelry, for gold was sacred to Aphrodite. Light candles at the altar. Say your own prayer to her, or read the verses of her most famous acolyte, the ancient Greek poet Sappho. Once more hold your personal mementos, and read the letters or look at the pictures. Close your eyes and remember those moments in your life of great passion. Tell Aphrodite that you are going to visit her sacred places and ask her to guide you on your journey. Ask her to smile upon you and bless you with love. If you can, let the candles burn as you begin your day. Otherwise, gently blow them out and leave them on the altar.

When you set out on your trip, make sure to take the clothes and jewelry you wore for the ritual so that you can wear them again when you enter her temple.

directions as the actual site. Sprinkle it with salt and water and a grain offering, and do a meditation to psychically connect your model to the Spirits of the site.

Take along spiritual aspects of your home as you travel. These might include something small from your altar, some grain or herbs grown in your area (the pot of sage I carry comes from a Shaker farm not far from my home), a special stone, or even a small jar of dirt from your garden. These things will help you form a link between the sacred places and your own life. Carry them and any other ritual objects or tools in a special bag, preferably one with a strap so you can carry it on your shoulder when you move about the site. If you decorate the bag in some way, either through embroidery or by drawing on it, or by attaching talismans or jewelry to it, you will personalize it so that it becomes part of your own ritual expression.

On Your Journey

As you travel, stay aware of the sacred nature of your journey. This does not mean you can't have fun browsing the local markets or spending the day at the beach. It does mean taking a few quiet moments each morning to think about your intentions.

Also, keep a journal of your experiences. Even if you write only a few sentences each day, you might find that insights and ideas come to you as you write. Include your dreams and any stray thoughts or significant events along the way. As an alternative or addition to writing, you could try drawing sketches of your travels.

What to Do at a Sacred Site

You've read about it and looked at pictures, studied the archaeological or historical information, and now you finally have arrived. Resist the temptation to rush about or frantically snap photos. Instead, take a moment to fully, ceremoniously,

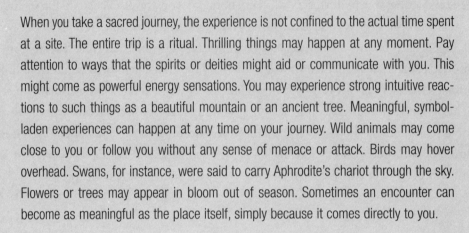

Omens and Signs

When you take a sacred journey, the experience is not confined to the actual time spent at a site. The entire trip is a ritual. Thrilling things may happen at any moment. Pay attention to ways that the spirits or deities might aid or communicate with you. This might come as powerful energy sensations. You may experience strong intuitive reactions to such things as a beautiful mountain or an ancient tree. Meaningful, symbol-laden experiences can happen at any time on your journey. Wild animals may come close to you or follow you without any sense of menace or attack. Birds may hover overhead. Swans, for instance, were said to carry Aphrodite's chariot through the sky. Flowers or trees may appear in bloom out of season. Sometimes an encounter can become as meaningful as the place itself, simply because it comes directly to you.

enter this special place. If you have traveled alone—and you do not mind tourists staring at you—you probably can do this as slowly and intensely as you like (short of disturbing other visitors by loud drumming and howling, or alarming guards by leaping about on the ruins). If you have come with a group, you still can take a few moments for a small private ritual before you join the lecture. The group leader also might enjoy your suggestion of an entrance ceremony.

Breathe deeply. Try to be aware of the ground under you and the energy it gives you. Feel the sky or roof above you. Listen to the sounds around you. Smell the fragrances in the air. Now, as your breathing goes deeper, let your mind drift back. Feel that you are following a very thin golden thread that will carry you back to the ancient times. Open your eyes. Say a blessing of gratitude for whoever and whatever have brought you here, and touch the Earth.

Now it is time to explore. Look around, follow your guide's lectures, take photos. If the literature does not mention directional alignments, check those with your compass, including alignments of any prominent landscape features, such as standalone mountains, cone-shaped hills, or sharp chasms. Often, guidebooks, and even some spiritual lecturers, simply will not mention such things, but you may find them as compelling as the actual structure itself.

Ceremonies at Sacred Sites

There is no general ritual to be held at any and all sacred sites. What you do depends on the place, the culture of the people who created it, the deities or Spirits involved, the season, and your own needs. Have you gone just to connect with the ancient energy? Have you gone for personal healing or transformation, or perhaps to seek help for others? Is it Summer or Winter, a time of rain or a time of drought? All these factors will shape your rituals. The examples of rituals throughout this book will help you shape what you want to do.

Finding Your Own Sacred Place

All the sacred places we have discussed were at one time "ordinary" spots until someone recognized them as special and then built a monument or a temple there, or just painted on the walls of a cave. You can recognize such places on your own, either alone or with a ritual group, and dedicate them to your own ceremonial use.

It often is easier to find a sacred space in nature. The energy that makes a place special will not disappear in a city, but all the activity will mask it. However, it is not impossible to find what you are looking for in a city park, or even, if you are sensitive enough, in a downtown area. Still, most people will want to go somewhere in nature. This does not mean hiking three days into wilderness. A rural area with mountains and woods, or a state park, will give you plenty of possibilities.

You may prefer to seek sacred places for their energy. You don't need an expensive piece of technology to detect this energy. You can find it through your own sensitivity.

Dowsing

One simple tool to find sacred energy is a dowsing stick, or divining rod. This is any forked stick that you hold by the two ends so that the straight end is pointed forward.

Dowsers famously find water. People who need a well dug in a difficult area will hire an experienced dowser, who often can tell them not only where to drill but how far down they will have to go. But you also can use a dowsing stick to locate that special charge of energy that marks a sacred site.

You can increase your innate dowsing ability by performing a simple ritual beforehand. Hold the stick loosely in your hands. Close your eyes and feel the Earth underneath you. Ask the Spirits or deities you follow to help you. Raise the stick to the sky, point it down at the ground, then point it straight out to the four directions. Finally, press it against yourself. Breathe deeply one more time, then open your eyes and begin to move around.

Hold the stick lightly and walk around. Try to stay in a meditative state and allow your intuition, rather than the conscious mind, to direct you.

When the rod reacts strongly and an energy charge passes through you, you will know you have found your place.

Symbolic Images from Nature

Subtle energy is not the only quality that makes a place special. Certain visual qualities in the land evoke the spiritual. A waterfall over a cave is an image that gives us awareness of divine energy. Chasms or deep holes in the Earth invite us to contemplate the secret depths within our own souls. Any place where an underground spring breaks through to the surface is a place of great energy.

Sacred places do not have to be as permanent as caves or even streams. A very old tree, one that is thick and twisted and with great character, can be a powerful image of divine energy. This is also true for multiple tree trunks. When such trees stand alone, or on top of a hill, they gain the power to unite the Earth and the sky through a living presence. A very great many religious and mythological traditions teach of a Tree of Life, or World Tree, whose roots are in the underworld, whose trunk stretches through our world of the senses, and whose branches disappear into the heavens. The fruit of such a tree is said to give immortal life. Any actual tree that can remind us of this cosmic Tree becomes a place of great sacred power.

To Dedicate a Sacred Place

Over and over in different spiritual traditions we see the idea that Spirits need humans to bring them into physical reality. The Jewish and Sufi mystical traditions both teach that God actually needs humans to witness His/Her acts, for without that witness God does not come fully into being. We even find a similar idea in modern science. The highly intellectual branch of physics known as quantum mechanics contains the idea that the entire universe exists only in a state of suspended probabilities until a conscious observer registers it. This "collapses" the probabilities into physical reality.

All this means that a "sacred place" is in fact only a place of energy. To truly become *sacred* a place needs someone to be present and perform a ritual. This can be as complicated or as simple as you like. The important thing is to create a human presence. One valuable way to formalize the relationship between the human and the sacred is to eat and drink something at the place you have found. Bread and wine are valuable because they are uniquely human creations out of the raw foods of nature. Fruit, on the other hand, honors the nourishment and delight we get from our mother, the Earth. Whatever you eat or drink, make sure to leave a small amount as an offering. This keeps the connection vibrant and alive.

Dedication is not something we do only at "unknown" sacred places. We also can do them at established temples and ruins and stone circles. If we treat them only as archaeological museum pieces, they will lose their divine truth. Each time a person or group rededicates them, their sacred power comes back to life.

Building a Sacred Site

Finding a place of power or natural energy is only one way to create a sacred site. A much more direct approach is simply to build something, either on your own property or at a center. Such constructions are like shrines, except that they are usually structures you can enter in some way.

Inspired by revival of interest in Stonehenge and other circles, people have begun to build their own miniature stone circles. Some of these can be quite large. Near my home in upstate New York stands a remarkable series of stone formations. The man who lives on this piece of land has actually quarried a section of it to bring up large dramatic stones. The biggest pieces stand by themselves, like prehistoric monoliths. One of them is a narrow pillar of rock, about six feet high. Other stones he balances on top of each other in formations of three or four. They do not form a circle but rather a kind of avenue of stones.

Other people have built sweat lodges, or laid out large Medicine Wheels based on one of the various American Indian designs. The labyrinth we described earlier is another way people create sacred space. In a way, what matters most about these creations is not their individual significance. More important is the fact that people in many places have begun to create a vision of the world as a carrier of spiritual wonder.

We have looked at many aspects of ritual. We have learned from religious traditions, we have seen how the senses contribute, and we have seen the special ways we use time and space. As we move toward the end of our journey through this book, we will consider ways in which ritual can help us with specific issues and give meaning to special moments in our lives.

⌒   RESOURCES   ⌒

BOOKS

Artress, Lauren. *Walking a Sacred Path: Rediscovering the Labyrinth As a Spiritual Tool.* New York: Riverhead, 1995.

Coleman, Simon and John Elsner. *Pilgrimage: Past and Present in the World Religions.* Cambridge, Mass.: Harvard University Press, 1995.

Milne, Courtney. *Sacred Places in North America.* New York: Stewart, Tabori & Chang, 1995.

Pollack, Rachel. *The Body of the Goddess.* Rockport, Mass.: Element Books, 1997.

Rossbach, Sarah. *Feng Shui: The Chinese Art of Placement.* New York: Dutton, 1995.

Wilson, Colin. *Atlas of Holy Places & Sacred Sites.* New York: DK, 1996.

VIDEO

Labyrinth: The History of the Maze. Available through Explorations (800–720–2114). See also www.gracecathedral.org for additional resources on the labyrinth and the work on Dr. Artress.

TOURS

Omega offers many tours to sacred sites yearly. Call 800–944–1001 for current trips.

The Institute of Noetic Sciences has an extensive travel program (800–353–2276).

The Four Winds Society (561–832–9702) focuses on shamanic power places.

Four

❖

Ritual
and You

9.

Special Uses of Ritual

The priestess and the minister stand side by side under the outdoor bower, a structure made of sticks taken from the ritual grove where the couple first met in a May Day ceremony. The minister has been part of one of the families for more than a generation. The priestess has helped guide the couple through many stages of their lives. The two of them, and the couple themselves, have spent hours together to craft a ceremony that will honor the couple's deep commitment to each other. Now the couple themselves come forward, strewn in flowers and bright ribbons that flash in the Sun. At the back of the ritual ground a fire burns, symbol of their desire to transform their separate lives and join together. At the end of the ceremony, they will hold hands and leap over the flames.

The sick woman lies on the hospital bed, a tray of medicines on one side of her, a vase of roses, red, the color of life, on the other side. On the windowsill stands a statue of Kwan Yin, Buddha of compassion. Tarot cards that show healing and wholeness are taped to the wall above the woman's head. All around the bed the circle of healers chants wordlessly. As the energy builds, the woman's brother, at the foot of the bed, asks the divine Healers for help. With each name—Kwan Yin,

Kwan Yin

Jesus, White Buffalo Woman, Krishna—he touches a drop of water from a crystal bowl onto his sister's forehead. At the peak of the chant all raise their arms, then bring them down to place their hands just above the woman's body. She smiles and breathes deeply for the first time in days.

What Ritual Can Do

We have looked at ritual as something done at certain times of the year or month, as ways to encounter the sacred at special places. Ritual is also very practical. It supports us when we make a major change, or when we struggle with some serious problem, such as illness, or a career change, or loneliness. Ritual can help us lead a child over the threshold into adulthood, or help an adult make a transition from divorce to a new life.

When we do a ritual for a special need, like healing, we allow powers beyond our own limitations to assist us. We call on them to move the energy of a situation, or release any blocks, or rekindle hope. The ritual does not replace our normal efforts. It reinforces them. At the very least, the ritual overcomes negativity in ourselves and focuses our own energy in productive ways. At the other end of the spectrum is the belief that the Spirits exist, and that they wish to help us. Ritual opens the gateway so that these beings can enter our world and bring whatever we urgently need.

Between these two views is the idea that any situation develops its own pattern, one that can become almost solidified in the world around us. Ritual breaks through such patterns and reshapes them.

Following are some special subjects for ritual. When we do such rituals, we are not trying to compel anyone to do anything. Rituals help us most when we use them to inspire our lives.

Healing—Rituals from Many Sources

The need for healing leads many people to seek help from ritual. Virtually every religious tradition has special ceremonies for the sick. When I was a child in a Jewish home, we lived across the street from a Catholic family. Whenever someone in our immediate or extended family became seriously ill, my father would go to the synagogue and ask the rabbi to say a special prayer before the Torah. At the same time, my mother would go across the street and ask the Catholic mother, Flora, to light a candle in the church for the sick person. If someone in Flora's family became sick, she went to the church and lit a candle to ask the Virgin Mary for help. And she also asked my father to have the rabbi say the prayer in the synagogue. When it comes to healing, both sides believed, you need all the help you can get.

Virgin Mary

Home Healing Rituals

You can do a simple ritual in your home for your own healing, or for someone else, whether the person lives with you or lives far away. The following suggestions are to send healing to someone else, but in fact they work equally well for yourself.

A Group Healing by a Hospital Bed

When someone has gone through surgery, or is sick enough to be in the hospital, often a group of friends and family might welcome the chance to call on sacred energy for the person's recovery.

Tell the nursing staff and any roommates (and their visitors) that you plan to do a simple healing ceremony.

Ask everyone ahead of time to think of what blessing they want to offer. As in the home ritual, children might enjoy drawing a picture of the person doing some healthy activity. Everyone also should bring some small token of the person, either something special the person gave them or a souvenir of a joyous activity they shared.

Clear the tray-on-wheels of the usual things that accumulate there. This becomes the altar space where you can set out the objects people have brought. Include something special to the sick person, such as a treasured set of rosary beads from childhood. The altar should include a bowl of water, fresh flowers, and fruit.

Everyone surrounds the bed. Begin the ritual with everyone breathing gently together. When you sense that everyone has become united, invoke whatever beings you want to aid the person. Say a blessing of gratitude, such as "We thank you for your presence. We ask that you add your grace to our love for _____. Listen as we share the many ways [he/she] blesses us."

Now each person shows the thing they have brought and explains what it means to them. They end with their own positive statements for the person's recovery. Finally, the sick person speaks of his or her own hopes and yearnings.

Say a prayer for healing. Here is a simple example: "Blessed Ones, bring perfect health to your son, _____. Fill him with strength and vitality so that he and his children ride together in the bright Sun. Heal his body, heal his soul. Heal his body, heal his soul. Heal his body, heal his soul." The third time, everyone joins in.

Thank the beings who have aided you. Once more, everyone speaks, just to say "We love you." Everyone shares the fruit.

We have looked at the idea of burning a long-lasting candle for a sick person. The ones sold in Hispanic sections of supermarkets (and some New Age stores) usually burn for about five days. Because a glass jar contains the entire candle, you can leave them burning (on the stove, or a metal tray or counter, away from sudden breezes) while you sleep or go out. Near the candle, but not against it, place a photo of the sick person, along with a written prayer for the person's recovery. A small bowl of water, changed daily, should go in front of the candle. If you do wish to invoke specific sacred beings, include a picture or symbol of them around the candle and photo. Unless you follow a particular tradition, or feel a strong attraction to one figure, you do not need to restrict yourself to a single image.

You can simply let the candle burn, or you can do a daily blessing before it. Chant the person's name, visualizing him or her in good health and doing some positive activity. If you do this with others, especially children, you all can discuss good things about the person, and the wonderful things she or he will do when healed. This ritual can be very helpful to children if someone they love—a parent or grandparent, a sibling, a friend—is very ill. Children might enjoy drawing a picture of the person doing some healthy activity. All of this works very well if you yourself are sick and want to involve your children in your healing.

End the ritual with a small bow to the person's photo and a simple blessing. Here is one I made up for a friend recovering from a long illness: "May you walk on the Earth in health and joy."

Something else you can do, for yourself or a friend, is to go to any nearby sacred site (including special trees or rocks on your own property or in a nearby park), make a small offering to the Earth, and say a blessing for the sick person.

Love Rituals

The world abounds with love charms, potions, talismans, and spells. While modern ritualists reject the idea of trying to compel someone to love you (it can do you more harm than good), you can do rituals to open yourself to love as well as to draw the right person to you.

Here is an example of such a "love spell."

1. Begin the ritual two days before the Full Moon. You will need a golden-colored bowl that you buy new and do not use for anything else. You will also need a red cup and two candles, a red one for desire and a white one for purity of purpose.

2. Find a photograph or picture that for you symbolizes love. It can be a couple you know and admire, your parents, a painting of great lovers, or a still from a movie. Put the picture in a gold frame.

3. Decorate an altar table or surface with red roses and white lilies intermingled. Place the candles, unlit, in candle holders on either side of the bowl. Set the framed picture behind the bowl. Fill the red cup with water and place it alongside the bowl.

4. Stand before the altar with palms together and look at the beauty of the things before you. Close your eyes and visualize the roses and lilies, the bowl, and the picture. See the altar radiant with the love you will have in your life.

5. Light the red candle and say, "Let this flame bring me a love that will burn with passion."

6. Light the white candle and say, "Let this flame bring me a love that is pure and true."

7. With the water from the red cup fill the bowl one-third full. Say, "As this water flows into this golden vessel, so love will flow into my life."

8. Close your eyes and visualize a lover walking toward you. Say, "I invite love into my life."

9. Stand before the altar a few minutes, then gently blow out the candles.

10. At the same time the next day repeat the ritual. This time, fill the bowl two-thirds full. Visualize a lover very close to you. Say, "I welcome love into my life."

11. On the third day, the day of the Full Moon, repeat the ritual and fill the bowl. Visualize your lover stepping into your arms for a passionate embrace. Say, "I accept love in all its beauty."

A Ritual for a New Home

Any time we move, but especially if we buy a house, we create new openings in our lives. Here is a ritual that acknowledges the hope that comes with a new home. Buy some rock salt, a hand mirror, a small tray, and bread, wine, and fruit, and do not take them inside the house. You also will need a small bowl you have brought from your old home, plus a rattle and any special objects of power that you have used in your old home or in rituals at centers or on journeys. Set everything outside on the front steps except the bowl. Place the sacred power objects and the food on the tray at the entrance. Now go inside and fill the bowl with water and carry it back outside (via a side or back door if possible; otherwise, step to the side so you do not step over the tray). Set the bowl before the objects as an offering for peace and good health. Before the bowl place the mirror. Mirrors were used in ancient times as charms to reflect any harm and prevent it from entering your house.

Now walk around the house clockwise, scattering small bits of rock salt as you go. Visualize the salt as a wall of protection. When you have returned to the front, pick up the rattle and once more walk around the house. Now, at each corner shake the rattle and ask all benevolent beings who are there to bless your home. Speak at each stop of what you want to experience in this house—love, family harmony, friendship, success, healing, whatever you feel most strongly.

When you reach the front again, place the rattle on the tray, pick up the tray, and carry it ceremoniously into the house. Lift the bread and speak of the birth of a new phase of your life. Eat a piece. Lift the wine and speak of the things that you bring with you that will be transformed. Drink a sip. Lift the fruit and speak of the wonderful joy and prosperity you will experience. Take a bite. Shake the rattle once more to thank the beings and end the ritual. If possible, leave the mirror and bowl of water outside for twenty-four hours.

12. Let the candles burn almost to the end, then put them out in water. Take the bowl outside and pour out the water. Say, "Love nourishes me." Finish with a seal, such as "amen" or "blessed be."

Rites of Passage

Rituals that honor, or allow, major changes in our lives, such as rites of adulthood, a wedding, or a funeral, help us change patterns. They acknowledge that we have replaced the old pattern, which no longer applies, with a new and more meaningful one. Without ritual we can become stuck in our old ways and beliefs even when a situation has changed.

Rites of passage also help other people adjust to our new selves. A marriage ceremony is not just for the couple. It helps their parents, families, and friends realize that the two separate people they have always known have now joined together. Phyllis Berman, director of the Elat Chayim Center for Jewish Renewal, says it is unfortunate that our culture seems to recognize so few rites of passage. Without some kind of meaningful puberty rites, for example, children not only find it difficult to cross over into adult life, their parents also find it very hard to give up the image of their sons and daughters as dependent children.

Expanding Our Rituals

Ritual can bring people together as it marks the major points of our lives. It allows us to communicate who we really are. There are traditionally four special areas that societies have marked for ritual—birth, puberty, (heterosexual) marriage, and death. In our time, these rites are quickly performed, and sometimes not at all. We tell everyone about a birth but do little of a ceremonial nature to signify how important it is. For years, the only common birth ritual were the cigars handed out by the father! Puberty—the coming-of-age for children—has become a private matter, even one we consider unnecessary to note, since sex education in schools now removes the need for any parent-child discussion of birds and bees. And death has become something the living are meant to get over quickly so they can get back to their daily lives.

When a child goes away to college, or gets a first job, he or she really is leaving home. Why not take notice of this event? When we move to a new house,

Celebrating a Girl's Coming-of-Age

A girl's first period is a very special moment, too often clouded over by shame or embarrassment. To make this a positive experience, many women have begun to organize rituals for their daughters' coming-of-age. Here is an example:

1. Invite a small group of sympathetic women of varied ages. Include one or two older teenagers, perhaps the girl's sisters or cousins.

2. The night before the ritual, the mother and daughter spend time together talking about their lives. One way to do this is to bake bread or cakes for the ritual. Include poppy seeds as a symbol of fertility.

3. If weather and setting permit, assemble outdoors by a stream of water. Bring the bread or cakes, several feet of red silk cord with a scissors, and red wine or juice with glasses for everyone. If possible, bring pomegranate juice. According to herbalist Fara Shaw Kelsey, the pomegranate is very high in phyto-estrogens, plant chemicals that are chemically similar to the female hormone.

4. Begin by pouring a small amount of the juice into the stream. As the water briefly turns red, speak of the flow of blood that carries through the generation of women.

5. Pour juice for each woman in turn. After she drinks, she talks to the girl about being a woman, whatever she wishes to share. When the girl's turn comes, she drinks and speaks about becoming a woman.

6. Now the mother winds the red cord around her daughter, the other women, and herself. The cord signifies the ties between women. The mother speaks of what it means for her that her child has come of age. Then she cuts the cord at each point between two of the participants, so that everyone has a length of cord to take home with her.

7. Share the bread or cakes to end the ritual.

especially if we move to a new community, we begin a new phase of life. Here, too, a ritual would encourage us to acknowledge how deep such changes go.

We celebrate weddings, so why not divorce? It may not be a joyous occasion, but it certainly marks a great change. Rituals do not have to express happy moments only. A funeral is sad, but very valuable. A divorce ritual can acknowledge the pain and sadness and anger; it can help us find the humor in the situation and get over the craziness that so many people feel at the breakup of a marriage.

As well as marriage and divorce, what of commitments to live together, or simply to enter into a serious relationship? All of these provide opportunities for rituals that bring people together and allow spiritual awareness to enter our lives and help us through our changes.

A Ritual for Menopause

More and more women have begun to acknowledge the great emotional significance when a woman ends her fertility and enters "cronehood." If you or someone you know is entering this phase of life, an example from Phyllis Berman may inspire you to create a ritual that will honor this particular time of passage.

Berman based her ceremony on a Jewish tradition, the custom of drinking four cups (of wine) at a Passover seder. She invited a group of women to drink four cups, each a different liquid, and tell a story with each one.

The first was sangria, for their experiences of first menstruation. The second cup, champagne, celebrated their first time of truly meaningful sex (not the loss of virginity, but sex as genuine emotion).

The third cup was milk. For this drink, the women talked of mothering. They described the birth of their babies, abortions or miscarriages, the bonds with their children, and what it was like to lose a child. Women who had never had children talked of what that had meant in their lives. The stories contained poignancy, sadness, humor. Such stories—of women's fierce passion for their children—are rarely told, not with the honesty the ritual allowed these women to share with each other.

Finally, they drank a cup of water, a symbol of the unknown. What would happen in their lives through menopause? What new worlds would they open? Only eight of the women had gone all the way through menopause. They spoke, and the other women absorbed their teachings.

The Western Way of Death

Possibly the most extreme "passage" that calls out for ritual is death. Death and birth are the great mysteries. Despite all the claims made over the centuries by the world's religious traditions, no one truly knows where we come from or where we go. We are left then with a recognition, and honoring, of the mystery itself. That, and our own grief. Funerals have a twofold purpose. They release the soul of the dead person to whatever journey it must take, and they allow the mourners to channel the overwhelming sorrow of losing someone they love.

In the West we have lost much of the meaning of funerals. We see them primarily as distasteful obligations. Morticians urge us to buy the most expensive coffins and arrangements, as a way to prove how much we loved the person. People cry, people make speeches, the body is buried, and then it is all supposed to be over. Well-meaning friends tell the mourners, "You have to go on with your life. He wouldn't want you to dwell on the dead." After two or three days, people are expected to be back at work at full performance.

The result of all this is anxiety, depression, irrational outbursts, confused feelings of abandonment, and guilt.

For an example of a truly meaningful funeral, we can look at the description Malidoma Patrice Somé gives in his book *Ritual.* A Dagara funeral, like all traditional death rites, is not just therapy for the mourners. It also helps the dead person make a proper journey. The funeral begins when a priest circles the house where the death has occurred with a ring of white ash. This prevents any evil spirits from entering the room where the priest and mourners will invoke the benevolent spirits who help the dead person "by squeezing enough emotion out of the hearts of the grievers." In this way, the "therapy" aspect of the funeral and the sacred become entwined. This is an essential wisdom of ritual funerals, that the expressions of grief actually help the dead spirit make its transition.

Everything in the Dagara funeral allows the experience of grief at the same time it carefully structures it. Adult funerals go on for three days and nights, adolescents for two, children for one. This does not mean that the people value children and adolescents less. Instead, the difference reflects the different involvements in society. An adult has gone through more life experiences, and as part of the funeral singers and musicians will tell the person's story. They sing to each other of the power of death and its meaning to humans.

The adult—and to a lesser extent the adolescent—has gone through initiation ceremonies and become part of a group. These experiences, too, must be honored. A person's initiation group will reenact his or her life, and even the history of the family up to the death they are mourning. All of this takes time, and allows for people to experience the complexities of their own relationships with the dead person.

At the end of the prescribed time, the grave diggers take the body to the burial area and lay it in a grave shaped like an egg. Most people are buried in nature, in graves that will blend in with the countryside. Elders, however, are often buried within the family compound, so that people can draw on the wisdom of someone who completed their tasks on Earth before passing to the other world. Such burial is a great honor.

Adapting Old Traditions

We do not need to accept Dagara or anyone's beliefs to benefit from their wisdom. We can adapt the sacred model of funerals to our own ways. If we follow a traditional religion, we can research the old ways of funerals and mourning and restore them—hopefully with the understanding of our own times. To prepare this way, and plan what we want to do, can be very helpful when we know that somebody is dying. If we do not wish to use any official religious system, we can invoke spirituality in our own way. For instance, if you find the phases of the Moon meaningful, you might want to hold a memorial on the first New Moon after the person's death, for the dark of the Moon has always symbolized the passage of dead souls to whatever will come next.

At a funeral, if the person owned something she or he considered very special, you could use this for a group blessing, in which everyone holds it for a time and speaks of their feelings for the person and what they would like to give the person for his or her journey. After everyone who wishes has spoken, the object can be placed with the body for burial or cremation.

Allow rituals to continue after the burial. For the first days after the death of a partner or close family member, make room for your grief. A daily ritual before your altar, or a gathering of a special circle of friends sometime after the funeral, will greatly help alleviate those deep feelings of pain, loss, and confusion.

Birth

At first, birth appears simply the opposite of death. One ends life and is filled with sorrow; the other begins it with great joy. They go together because they both confront us with mystery. What lies beyond the world we know? What comes before life as well as after it? For many years I have thought that when children ask "Where do babies come from?" they are not trying to find out about the mechanics of sexual reproduction but instead are asking the ultimate question. Where *do* babies come from? How do a sperm and an egg become a living being, with its own unique qualities, its own soul? A ritual that honors birth needs to express this mystery as well as the happiness of the family.

Here, as in so many other areas, our culture leaves us with few guidelines. We simply have lost the habit of properly marking such major moments with ritual. One thing we might consider is that the proper time for a baby ritual is not necessarily right after the birth, when the mother is worn out and needs to rest and to be with her baby. Instead, many traditions plan for some ceremony, such as baptism in a church, some days later.

Burying the Placenta

There is one very old ritual some people still follow immediately or shortly after a birth. This is to bury the placenta. Often a midwife will do it; sometimes the mother will save it until she is strong enough to do it herself, along with the father, or possibly a circle of friends. If you do choose to follow this custom, do it with proper sacred understanding and ceremony. Such a burial is really an offering to the Earth, our first mother. It acknowledges that we are part of nature, that even as a child emerges into the world of humans it belongs to the Earth as well. As a Wiccan chant puts it, "We all come from the goddess, And to her we shall return." Another holy verse we might quote: "Dust you are, and to dust you shall return"—not as a counsel of despair or even humility, but really a statement of our oneness with all life.

Naming Ceremonies

One custom that has started to become popular is a ritual to give a newborn child its name. This can be done at a church or ritual center, but also at home. It should be a time of celebration and feasting, but also of proper solemnity. Many of the ritual foods we have discussed will be useful here. Fresh baked bread symbolizes the birth itself. Wine or juice signifies that the soul or Spirit of the child may have gone through many journeys, many lifetimes, before this one. Fruit represents abundance and prosperity. Finally, we should not forget milk and honey, the foods that signify motherhood and the sweetness of life.

Beforehand, ask everyone to bring some small gift that will symbolize what they would like this child to receive or experience in life. Make sure to include any brothers or sisters old enough to follow the idea; even if they are too young to fully understand, they should take part. The parents should discuss the name they have chosen before the ritual. Does it have a special meaning? Most of the common names in English actually have a literal meaning, usually in Latin or Hebrew.

A good dictionary (or baby book) will include the meanings of commonplace names. If the parents are naming the child after a relative, why have they chosen that person?

Begin the ceremony with the guests in a circle holding hands around the mother, father, and baby. Brothers and sisters also stand in the center. The parents speak of the name and what it means, and what they hope for the baby. Next, the other children give their gifts.

As each guest presents the object they have chosen, they call on whatever deity or tradition they themselves follow to give the child a gift. "I ask Jesus, Son of the compassionate God, to bless you with kindness and mercy." "I ask Oshun, orisha of love, to bless you with great emotion and the openness to express it." People who do not feel an attachment to any tradition might say something like "I ask the mystery of life to bless you with wonder."

When everyone has spoken, the person who baked the bread brings it forth and speaks of its symbolism. Then the other ritual foods are shared, as a bridge between the ceremony and the simple joy of celebration.

These are only a few of the many ways we create rituals to mark special situations or changes in our lives. They incorporate the various discoveries we have made about ritual and its meanings. Now we will take a final look at how you can bring all these aspects together in your own ritual practice.

✑ RESOURCES ✑

BOOKS

Achterberg, Jeanne, Barbara Dossey, and Leslie Kolkmeier. *Rituals of Healing.* New York: Bantam, 1994.

Berman, Phyllis. *Tales of Tikkun: New Jewish Stories to Heal the Wounded World.* Northvale, N.J.: Jason Aronson, 1996.

Budapest, Zsuzsanna E. *The Grandmother of Time.* San Francisco: HarperSanFrancisco, 1989. (See also Budapest's *Summoning the Fates: A Woman's Guide to Destiny,* Harmony Books, 1998, for life passage rituals.)

Dolnick, Barrie. *Simple Spells for Love.* New York: Harmony Books, 1995.

Horrigan, Bonnie. *Red Moon Passage: The Power and Wisdom of Menopause.* New York: Crown, 1997.

Linn, Denise. *Sacred Space: Clearing and Enhancing the Energy of Your Home.* New York: Ballantine, 1995.

Somé, Malidoma Patrice. *Ritual.* New York: Penguin, 1993.

Weed, Susun. *Menopausal Years: The Wise Woman Way.* Woodstock, N.Y.: Ash Tree, 1992.

AUDIO

Halifax, Joan. *Being with Dying.* Sounds True Audio.

10.
Your Own Ritual Practice

It's late afternoon in the middle of May. You're sitting in the kitchen, drinking a cup of tea, and looking out at the fresh flowers that have recently bloomed all around the shrine to rebirth you created in your rock garden at the beginning of Spring. Incense from the small kitchen altar mingles with the fresh breezes from outside.

The phone rings. Your sister is on the line. She tells you that she and a group of friends were reading about Solstice celebrations and they think it would be a lovely thing to do with their families. Would you be willing to lead a ritual for them? You smile. Your mind goes back to bonfires late at night, to chants and dances and fireworks. You begin to think of ways to guide them so they feel safe, and still make sure everyone has a chance to participate. "I'd love to," you say.

Looking Back

We have looked at ritual from many sides in this book: the secular and the spiritual, its sacred meanings, its emotional benefits. We have seen how different tra-

The Many Names of the Divine

Through our explorations of the world's ritual traditions we have encountered specific religious images. While some people want such an attachment to the ways humanity has expressed the sacred, others may feel uncomfortable with figures from established religions. We can, if we wish, address the divine in names that do not belong to any particular culture. Here are some examples:

Source of Life

Mother/Father of All Beings

Radiant Ones

Bright Beings

Beloved

Gracious One

Father of Truth, Mother of Kindness (or the reverse)

Father of Wisdom

Guardian of the Way

Wise Ones

Keepers of the Heart

Shaper of Souls

Protector

Thread of Our Lives

Mother of Oceans, Mother of Life

Lord of Justice

Hand of Compassion

ditions approach the divine through varied ways, and we have explored the possibilities for ritual in our own lives. We have discovered the basic idea of ritual, that it does not force anything to happen but instead invites the power of sacred energy to enter our world and our experience. Malidoma Somé says, "We cannot make sacred. The sacred is made by the spirits themselves." We can, however, make openings.

Through all the teachings we have discussed, we have looked at how we can translate the ideas into our own experiences. Such tools as the bell of the Buddhists can aid all of us in creating rituals that will touch us on deep levels. The Jewish Sabbath becomes an example of gentle rest that can benefit everyone. We have seen how to heal with ritual, how to invite love into our lives, how travel can become a sacred journey to our own truth.

In this last chapter, we will consider a basic outline for your own ritual practice, as well as some further special ways to use ritual in your life.

A Template for Ritual

Longtime ritualist Mary Greer has developed a general pattern for personal ritual that can help you. Here are her steps to ritual, slightly shortened (and paraphrased) from her book *The Essence of Magic*:

1. Intent. You should clearly state what you hope to accomplish, what you want to transform or create.

2. Preparation. Consider the time, such as the season or Moon cycle. What kind of altar do you want to create? Has a particular myth inspired you? If so, reread it before the ritual.

3. Gather everything you need.

4. Purify yourself and the space. We have seen how methods include smudge sticks, incense, a bath for yourself, salt water, or shaking a rattle in the room.

5. Create a sacred circle. This does not have to mean marking out an actual circle on the floor. You may simply invoke the four directions and visualize a circle, or bubble of energy, around you.

6. Invoke the presence of whatever power(s) you wish to help you. This can be a specific being from myth or religion, your personal guides, or any of the general names just cited. State your purpose out loud and bless any tools. Greer suggests that you can say out loud why you have chosen this or that object, and what it means to you.

7. The work. You may feel the need to banish something before you create. To let go of old patterns or unwanted energy you can act out the release, or chant/breathe it away, or write it on paper and burn it. You may need to cry or acknowledge old wounds. Follow this with a statement of release and healing, such as "I let go of the pain of my failed relationship. I know I did what I needed to do. I move freely into my new life."

   Now you can create. Have a clear image of what you want and back it up with stories and myths, visualizations, songs, written affirmations or blessings, creation of drawings or talismans. Involve as many senses as possible (part of the preparation is having things to touch and taste and smell that will symbolize your purpose).

8. Charge the work. One way to do this is to imagine a cone of energy over you and all that you have done.

9. Ground the energy. Use your arms and hands, and perhaps a wand or knife, to channel the energy down and touch the ground or floor. This helps make it real in your life.

10. Sit quietly for "silent thanksgiving." As you sit, you may realize some aspect that you have not finished, a chant you want to sing, a blessing to say, an affirmation to write.

11. Thank and dismiss whatever beings or energies you have invoked.

12. Open the circle. If you originally called on the powers of the four directions, release them.

A Special Ritual Tool

If you're a person who likes to sew or do handicrafts, you might enjoy making some sort of ritual garment, such as a robe, or jacket, or shawl that contains objects of your personal power. You do not actually have to sew the original piece of clothing (though it may carry more power for you if you do). You can buy something that you like, preferably something simple, and then add to it so that it becomes your creation. You might draw or paint on it, pin things to it, sew on ribbons in symbolic colors, attach pockets or pouches to hold written prayers, special stones, herbs or tinctures, your knife (or compass). Let your imagination play with the possibilities. Unlike a medicine bundle, which some people like to wear in many situations (for personal power and to carry the sacred with them), you probably will want to wear your robe or jacket only in rituals. Each ritual you do with it will increase its power and its meaning for you.

13. Review the ritual soon afterward, and then a little further on. Consider what worked well for you and what you would change next time.

Feel free to modify this model in any ways that will make it more helpful to you.

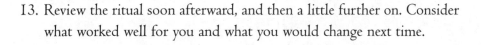

Divination and Sacred Energy

A number of times in this book we have looked at moments when you might want to use Tarot cards or some other form of divination. Besides Tarot cards, popular divination systems include Runes (magical letters from ancient alphabets of Northern Europe), the I Ching (a very old Chinese form of divination; its text is said to be the oldest book in the world), palmistry, tea leaves, and of course astrology. Recently, less well known but very meaningful divination systems have become more available to a popular audience through kits and instruction books. These include *Ifa*, the divination system of West Africa, and *Ogham*, a Celtic "tree alphabet." Some techniques, such as "scrying" or "gazing" into a crystal or a bowl of water, do not use any system of meanings but rely solely on the power of intuition.

We do not have the space here to look at methods or even a detailed description for these many kinds of divination. Luckily, there are good books available for all of them. What we can do is look at ritual approaches to divination in general. The term "divination" derives from "divine," for people originally used all these techniques to allow the gods to communicate with them. Many people who do Tarot or crystal gazing or any of the others find they get much better results when they first align themselves with sacred energy. We should stress that most modern diviners and readers do not try to predict the future (and definitely not control others in any way). Instead, they use these methods for greater awareness of who they are, what has brought them to their current situation, and what choices they face.

Rituals for Divination

Many people like to keep their divination tools in some ritualized way that reminds them that these tools are special. An old tradition says to wrap Tarot cards in a silk scarf. You can tie the scarf with a ribbon and attach a pendant or some other symbolic object to the ribbon's ends. If you use a large scarf, when you open it you can lay it out as an altar for the reading. Others keep their divination tools in a wooden box that also may hold crystals, stones from a sacred journey, or some symbolic object. They, too, may use a special cloth for an altar. In choosing such items as an altar cloth or a box for your tools, indulge yourself. Get something you really like. We underestimate the power of beauty to awaken our intuition.

As we have seen, an altar can hold many spiritual symbols, from a family photograph to a statue. For divination you might want your altar to include some central symbol of enlightenment, such as a large crystal and, of course, the actual divination tools.

One way to organize an altar is through the directions and the elements. Tarot, astrology, and magic all follow the ancient system of four elements that summarize the basic issues of life. Very briefly, Fire represents action and inspiration, Water emotion and intuition, Air thought, and Earth physical reality. We can align these elements to the directions with a symbolic object at each point. In the East, a candle can represent Fire. A feather, or the smoke of incense, indicates Air in the North. In the West we place a stone for the Earth. A small bowl of Water goes in the South.

Dreams

Our dreams fascinate us. Charged with emotion, strange, sad or wildly funny, embarrassing, they take us to another world every night while we sleep. Some of us remember our dreams vividly; others steadfastly believe they never dream at all. In fact, sleep researchers have found that literally everyone dreams, several times a night. It would seem that dreams are one of the main reasons for sleep.

Today, many people seek to remember and understand their dreams. They keep a dream journal alongside the bed so they can write down everything before they forget it. They go to dream workshops or therapists to try to find the messages their unconscious is trying to tell them. Many ancient and indigenous peoples saw dreams as messages from the divine. Sometimes these messages gave prophetic information, as in the biblical story of Joseph, who understood Pharaoh's dream of seven fat cows and seven lean ones as a warning that after seven good harvest years would come seven years of famine. Other times dreams brought healing, or instructions of what offerings to make to the gods to restore health or bring prosperity. Today people seek knowledge in dreams of what they need to do to improve their lives.

Peter Lamborn Wilson, in a wonderful small book called *Shower of Stars: Dream and Book*, describes how the Sufis and Taoists and others saw dreams as a path to initiation. That is, in certain dreams, higher beings would appear to the person to lead him or her to knowledge, spiritual transformation, or healing.

A Ritual for Diviners

1. Begin the ritual with a purification. You might want to use a smudge stick, or sprinkle salt water or spray diluted essential oil in the air.

2. Unwrap your divination tools and spread the cloth if you are using one for your altar. Place the cards, or Runes, or whatever you've chosen, in the center, along with any tools or symbolic objects.

3. When you have set everything up, close your eyes and take a few breaths to center yourself. If you follow a particular tradition that includes a deity of divination, envision that figure. See him or her sitting across from you. If you do not wish to invoke a special being, simply ask the Spirit of Wisdom to guide you.

4. Now align yourself to the directions. You can set out objects or simply visualize them. If you are reading for someone else, you can explain the symbolism of what you are doing or simply tell them you wish to center yourself. From the North ask for clear thought. From the East, look for inspiration. From the South, compassion; from the West, honesty. To these four points add Above for truth, Below for strength, and the Center for balance. Do not rush through this process. When you have taken in all seven, sit once more and breathe. Then open your eyes. You are ready to begin.

5. Do the reading. Give it the time and attention it needs.

6. When you have finished, take a few moments to sit quietly and see if anything further comes to you. When you sense that you have come to a rest with the work, take a deep breath to end the reading. Thank whatever guides you have asked to help you.

Not all dreams have these special qualities. Modern people who work with dreams have rediscovered an ancient truth: Most dreams do not carry the weight of special messages, prophecies, healing, or enlightenment. Many dreams are simply a release of the day's leftover worries and stimulations. Some dreams are even entertainment. But there are those others—the ones where we wake up with the knowledge, and sometimes the fear, that some great truth has come to us.

Dream Incubation

There is a ritual you can use to ask for a meaningful dream. It is called an "incubation," as if we hatch the dream from an egg. You can do this in your own bedroom.

You will need to sleep alone for this, so if you sleep with a spouse or partner, either ask them to use a guest room or do so yourself. Prepare the room well before sleep. Clean it, wash the bedding so everything is fresh, and open the window if weather permits. If the room already contains an altar, make sure it includes fresh water and flowers, along with any statues or images that suggest inner guidance. An example might be a meditating Buddha. Include as well something very personal, such as a piece of jewelry from a parent or grandparent. If there is no altar in the room, create a simple one with such objects. You might want to place an American Indian "dreamcatcher" on the wall over the bed. These are decorative wooden hoops with a kind of webbing inside them to attract good dreams. You can find these in many spiritual or New Age stores.

Before the day of the ritual, look around for any small stone with a hole in it. An old tradition calls these "dreamstones," as if the hole opens to the world of dreams. A dreamstone is not necessary for incubation, but if you are lucky enough to find one, pass a colored ribbon—blue for wisdom, red for strength, green for health—through it so that you can wear it around your neck while you sleep.

Tell any other people in the house that you are doing a special ritual for dreams and that you will need some time alone, and in quiet, before you go to sleep. Make sure you thank them for their cooperation.

Wash yourself. Take a bath if possible, slowly, with the sense that you are entering a ritual dream temple. If you sleep in pajamas or a nightgown, make sure everything is freshly washed.

When you go into the room, purify the room with sprinkled salt water or a smudge stick. If you have found a dreamstone, put it on now. Bow once to your altar and once to your bed. Now it is time to lie down.

Turn off the light and lie peacefully (if, like me, you have stacks of books alongside the bed, move them out for this night). Breathe quietly and let yourself drift into sleep.

You may not dream a truly powerful dream the first time you do this. Peter Lamborn Wilson comments that in Japan people would travel to a dream temple and make a commitment to sleep there up to a hundred nights in the hope of having a sacred dream. With the pace of our world, most people will not want to do a dream ritual for more than three nights in a row. If you do wake up that first time and feel nothing much has happened, thank the dream spirits anyway and ask them to return that night.

When you do have your special dream—and you will know it the moment you wake up—write it down so that you do not forget any of the details. Write down your reactions and any thoughts of what it means or ideas of what you might need to do. Thank all the spirits and the dream itself. That evening,

Offerings

A number of times in this book we have mentioned offerings. In old ritual traditions this often meant an animal sacrifice. For our modern context we have talked of leaving out part of the ritual food for animals, or pouring water onto the Earth. There is another kind of offering we can make in gratitude to the sacred powers, and that is charity. If you have done a ritual for a special purpose, you might want to give money to some organization connected to the ritual's intent. For example, if you did a ritual in hopes of getting pregnant, you could make a donation to a children's home or hospital. If you borrow something from American Indian tradition, such as the Vision Quest, think of giving some money to an organization for Native American rights, or to an educational fund.

Another thing to offer is time. Volunteer at a school or some other local place that could use help. Again, you would reinforce the ritual if you gave your time to a place or organization that did something that related to your ritual.

before you get ready for bed in your regular way, say a blessing of gratitude one last time at your dream altar.

Blessings

Most of us who went to traditional churches or synagogues as children grew up with the belief that only a priest or minister or rabbi could give a blessing. This was not just some special power they had—they were trained to do it. If any of us tried it, we simply would not know what to do.

Often in this book we have seen moments that called for a blessing. I have given various examples. Anyone can do this. At the proper moment in the ritual, open yourself to whatever needs to come through you. See yourself as a channel for the energy that *wants* to bless the altar, or the Earth, or the Spirits. You do not need to compose grand poetry. You just need an openness to let it happen.

To bless someone else is a wonderful experience. It makes you feel of true value. Even though *you* are not doing it, as in the conscious ego, it still is you, so that as you open yourself to the blessing that wants to help that person, you discover the real experience of sacred power moving through your body and spirit. Again, you do not need any special talent to bless someone. An openness to the person as well as the energy is all that it requires.

Some blessings will go just from you to the other person. Other blessings will be mutual, with each of you speaking. If someone is sick, or very distressed, let the blessing you give them be its own reward.

When you bless someone in trouble, do not fake anything. You are not there to reassure them that everything will be fine. Instead, simply allow whatever is strong and positive to emerge. You will receive back their emotions, especially the sense of hope and peace that genuine belief can create.

In other situations, a mutual blessing will allow each person to give as well as receive. You might do this as part of a larger ritual or ceremony. If you celebrate the Spring Equinox with a friend, the two of you might decide to bless each other. In large groups, you can do it in pairs (with one group of three if there is not an

How to Bless Someone

Begin with you and the other person holding hands and looking into each other's eyes. Both of you close your eyes and breathe quietly until you feel yourselves breathing together. Open your eyes and look at each other.

There are two basic ways to bless someone. For the first way, ask the person what she or he needs. Listen carefully, with full attention. Then allow yourself to respond to what the person has told you. If the person says, "I want to meet someone for a serious relationship," you might find yourself moved to say, "May the Keepers of the Heart open your heart to love. May the right partner walk into your life and may the two of you discover harmony and passion, commitment and joy. May the love that fills the universe grow in both of you. May it be so." If you like, you could end with "Amen" or "Blessed be" or some other seal.

The second approach involves your own intuition. Intuition is not so much a skill as an opening. Anyone can do it. All it takes is willingness. Look into the other person and let intuition reveal what the person truly needs. Try not to make this an ego judgment, as in "I think this person looks very sad and lonely. I think he needs a partner." Instead, let the blessing flow through you. You might say to someone sorrowful, "May your life amaze you with happiness. May courage to move forward come to you in all difficult moments. May love appear for you and bring you joy."

even number of people). You and someone else also might choose to bless each other at some special moment, such as the first time you become lovers with a partner, or if you and a friend go through some special experience together.

A Blessing for This Book

To write (and also to read) a book, especially one about spirituality, is a kind of ritual all by itself. We travel through the book like a pilgrimage, stopping at the different teachings the way we would visit sacred sites. In our look at the varied traditions we have invoked guides and deities many times, through their images and stories, and especially through the dedicated teachers whose knowledge we have gone to like deep wells for the nourishment of their wisdom and example.

It seems fitting to end this book with a final blessing. Rather than make up something entirely new, I have followed the advice of a couple of friends who suggested I include a passage from an earlier book of mine. Here, then, is a modified version of that passage:

> *Open your heart to the Sun. Open your eyes to the Sky. Open your ears*
> *to the Sea. Deep love to the round Earth who has given us bodies.*
> *Deep love to the stars for their energy and light. Deep love to our*
> *mothers and fathers for the gene patterns of our souls.*
> *Deep love to our mothers, for the home of our first growth.*
> *We bless each other for the truths we have shared.*
> *We are people of love. We are people of bone. We are blessed.*
> *We are people of light. We are people of words. We are blessed.*
> *We are people of truth. We are blessed.*
> *May it be so.*

✐   RESOURCES   ✐

BOOKS

Biziou, Barbara. *The Joy of Ritual: Spiritual Recipes to Celebrate Milestones, Ease Transitions, and Make Every Day Sacred.* New York: Golden Books Adult, 1999.

Greer, Mary K. *The Essence of Magic.* Van Nuys, Calif.: Newcastle, 1993.

Matthews, John. *The World Atlas of Divination.* New York: Little Brown, 1992.

Pollack, Rachel. *Temporary Agency.* New York: St. Martin's Press, 1994.

Wilson, Peter Lamborn. *Shower of Stars: Dream and Book.* Autonomedia, 1996.

THE FOLLOWING BOOKS AND DIVINATION SETS GIVE
DETAILED INFORMATION ON VARIOUS ESOTERIC
SYMBOL SYSTEMS THAT CAN BE USED IN RITUAL

Blum, Ralph. *The Book of Runes.* New York: St. Martin's Press, 1982.

Carr-Gomm, Philip and Stephanie. Illustrated by Bill Worthington. *The Druid Animal Oracle.* New York: Fireside, 1994.

Carson, David and Jamie Sams. Illustrated by Angela Wernke. *Medicine Cards.* Santa Fe, N. Mex.: Bear & Co., 1988.

Casey, Caroline. *Making the Gods Work for You: The Astrological Language of the Psyche.* New York: Harmony Books, 1988.

Dening, Sarah. *The Everyday I Ching.* New York: St. Martin's Press, 1995.

Noble, Vicki. *Making Ritual with Motherpeace Cards.* New York: Three Rivers Press, 1998.

Smoley, Richard. *Hidden Wisdom: A Guide to the Western Inner Traditions.* New York: Penguin, 1999.

Index

B

C